Edited by SAMUEL KIR\

G000152934

ADVISING IN AUSTERITY

Reflections on challenging times for
advice agencies

POLICY PRESS SHORTS POLICY & PRACTICE

First published in Great Britain in 2017 by

Policy Press
University of Bristol
1-9 Old Park Hill
Bristol
BS2 8BB
UK
+44 (0)117 954 5940
pp-info@bristol.ac.uk
www.policypress.co.uk

North America office:
Policy Press
c/o The University of Chicago Press
1427 East 60th Street
Chicago, IL 60637, USA
t: +1 773 702 7700
f: +1 773 702 9756
sales@press.uchicago.edu
www.press.uchicago.edu

© Policy Press 2017

British Library Cataloguing in Publication Data
A catalogue record for this book is available from the British Library.

Library of Congress Cataloging-in-Publication Data
A catalog record for this book has been requested.

ISBN 978-1-4473-3414-9 (paperback)
ISBN 978-1-4473-3416-3 (ePub)
ISBN 978-1-4473-3417-0 (Mobi)

The right of Samuel Kirwan to be identified as the editor of this work has been asserted by him in accordance with the Copyright, Designs and Patents Act 1988.

Cover design by Policy Press
Front cover: image kindly supplied by Christopher Heppell
Printed and bound in Great Britain by CMP, Poole
Policy Press uses environmentally responsible print partners

Contents

Notes on contributors

This book was made possible by the generous and thoughtful contributions of our research participants. All of the names used when citing participants, or recounting their experiences, are pseudonyms.

Gail Bowen-Huggett is a Trustee for the South West Legal Support Trust and a Radio Presenter for Ujima Radio working to ensure that access to justice is available to all. Following a successful commercial career, Gail turned her attention to the Third Sector in 2004 when she joined Bristol Debt Advice Centre (now Talking Money). She then became involved with ACFA: The Advice Network and most recently acted as Advice Development Coordinator for a project funded by the Advice Services Transition Fund (ASTF), alongside completing an MSc in Strategy, Change and Leadership at University of Bristol.

Nicole Busby is Professor of Labour Law at the University of Strathclyde. In her research she explores labour market regulation and its socioeconomic context. Her recent work focuses on the relationship between paid work and unpaid care, the constitutionalisation of labour rights and claimants' experiences of the UK's Employment Tribunal system.

John Clarke is a Professor Emeritus in Social Policy at the Open University and also teaches at Central European University in

Budapest. He has written extensively about welfare states, public services and citizenship. For many years he was a CAB trustee.

Sue Evans is Director of Bristol Citizens Advice, and has an in-depth knowledge of advice work, having spent the last 28 years managing a variety of independent third sector and statutory advice services.

Michael Ford QC is Professor of Law, University of Bristol and a fee-paid Employment Judge. He is Counsel for the Equality and Human Rights Commission in the judicial review case challenging the legality of Employment Tribunal fees.

Jennifer Harris started her PhD at the University of Bristol in 2012 and is also employed as a researcher at Caring in Bristol. Based at three different homelessness support organisations, Jennifer's PhD research explored how homeless people are using technology to access resources within the context of the current shift to digital advice and welfare benefit provision. Jennifer's interest in this field stems from her previous employment in various related fields, namely as a housing officer, a researcher on a hidden homelessness project, a Gateway Assessor at a Citizens Advice Bureau, and as a regular volunteer at a Christmas Shelter.

Eleanor Kirk is a researcher at the University of Bristol Law School. Whilst working on the 'Employment Disputes' project she was also completing her PhD on how conflict is expressed in the contemporary workplace, how workers' grievances come to be focused on particular issues, and the role therein of collective organisation. Eleanor lives in Glasgow.

Samuel Kirwan is a research fellow at the University of Warwick who worked on the New Sites of Legal Consciousness project. He is particularly interested in the process of money advice, and the moral language of debt and credit that surrounds it, and has a longstanding interest in the concept of the commons.

Alison Kite has recently completed a PhD on the delivery of Citizens Advice services in GP surgeries. Before this she worked in the voluntary sector and in local government. She has been interested in advice work since the 1990s when she trained as a volunteer with Citizens Advice before becoming a welfare rights adviser with a local charity.

Morag McDermont is Professor of Socio-Legal Studies in the University of Bristol. In 2011 she was awarded a research grant by the European Research Council for 'New Sites of Legal Consciousness: a case study of UK advice agencies'. Morag has previously worked in local government and the housing association sector.

Joe McGlade – Having worked in various jobs, on returning to Northern Ireland in 2001 Joe McGlade volunteered with Citizens Advice, where he has been a Generalist Adviser and Tribunal Representative for 15 years. He holds specialisms in anti-discrimination and employment law casework. Here Joe reflects upon Brian's case study as both the holder of a law degree and as an adviser with many years' experience of dealing with clients' employment disputes.

Emily Rose is a Lecturer in the School of Law at the University of Strathclyde. Her main area of research interest is labour law and social aspects of work and organisations. Emily's academic background spans both law and sociology and this interdisciplinary perspective informs the work she undertakes.

Adam Sales is a sociologist who has carried out previous research exploring power inequalities in relation to health, education and law, using the thinking of Pierre Bourdieu. He was a Research Associate on the 'Citizens Advice Bureaux and Employment Disputes' project.

List of acronyms

Acas: The advice, conciliation and arbitration service
ACFA: (Formerly) Advice Centres For Avon
ADR: Alternative Dispute Resolution
ASTF: Advice Services Transition Fund
BIS: Department of Business, Investment and Skills
CAB(x):   Citizens Advice Bureau(x)
CAS: Citizens Advice Scotland
CitA: Citizens Advice (England and Wales)
CLSP: Community Legal Service Partnership
CSP: Customer Service Point
DWP: Department for Work and Pensions
ESA: Employment and Support Allowance
ET: Employment Tribunal
ET1:   The initial form required to begin an Employment
            Tribunal procedure.
GP: General Practitioner
HR: Human Resources
ICT: Information and Communications Technology
JCP: Job Centre Plus
JSA: Job Seeker's Allowance
LA: Local Authority
LASPO: Legal Aid, Sentencing and Punishment of Offenders Act
            (2012)
LSC: Legal Services Commission

MoJ:	Ministry of Justice
NAPO:	Probation and Family Court Union
UC:	Universal Credit

INTRODUCTION

Samuel Kirwan, John Clarke, Morag McDermont and Alison Kite

Increasing numbers of people in the United Kingdom find themselves needing advice and support in dealing with a growing range of problems. Whether it is a dispute with one's employer, a stop on one's benefit payments, an impending eviction, or a default on a debt, the background to this book is the rising number of individuals with 'civil law' issues that can rapidly lead to situations of crisis. These growing problems have a troubled relationship to the current period of 'austerity'. Presented alongside an increasingly familiar narrative of 'tightening our belts' and 'living within our means', a series of policies pursued by UK governments since 2010 have intensified such problems, while the reductions in public funding that they have mandated, most notably to the Civil Legal Aid budget, have reduced the range and scope of many public organisations to offer advice or support. At the same time, there has been an expectation that voluntary organisations would somehow 'fill the gap' left by the withdrawal of public services – an expectation exemplified in David Cameron's image of the 'Big Society'. As a consequence, voluntary organisations providing advice and support find themselves at a particularly acute junction of these social and economic pressures – while facing problems of their own, not least reductions in their funding as the 'austerity' cuts work their way through the funding system.

This book explores this conjunction of needs and pressures around advice. It is particularly concerned with how people's troubles bring them into contact with advice agencies, and with the relationship between those troubles and the official worlds of policy and law: for example, how does the experience of being unjustly treated at work become a legal matter? The relationship between law and justice is a critically important one for many of these troubles – whether they are matters of immigration, housing, benefits, indebtedness or redundancy. The book emerges from the 'New Sites of Legal Consciousness' Research Programme. Based at the Universities of Bristol and Strathclyde and running between 2012 and 2015, it set out to understand the world of advice and its relationship to the law. The focus on advice and law is one way of capturing the wide-ranging political and social changes in this period that shaped the changing *need* for advice and the increasing difficulties encountered by the public in dealing with the problems they faced.

We have called the book 'Advising in Austerity' as a way of identifying the current political period – a period characterised by concerted attempts to shift the relationship between the individual and the state in the name of economic necessity. However, our use of the term 'austerity' does not mean we think it is a credible description of the claimed economic necessity, nor is it even a particularly accurate term for describing the policies pursued by UK governments since 2010. Indeed, inasmuch as 'austerity' indicates a conservative caution with managing the 'public purse' (aka 'living within our means'), claims a spirit of solidarity that transcends wealth and class (aka 'we are all in this together'), and celebrates an ethic of saving rather than accruing debts, it bears little relation to current social and economic policy (see the discussions in Evans and McBride, forthcoming; Clarke and Newman, 2012; Wren-Lewis, 2015). It may be more helpful to think of current policies as being legitimated or authorised by the *idea* of 'austerity' – a 'dangerous idea', as Mark Blyth calls it (Blyth, 2013; see also Levitas, 2012). These policies have deepened and extended existing tendencies, which can be grouped with others under the label of 'neo-liberalism', including dismantling protection, stability and security in the employment and private housing spheres; cutting welfare entitlements to the bare minimum required for survival coupled with a stigmatisation of claimants; and the encouragement of unsecured debt as a way of making ends meet in the context of stagnating wages (see Peck, 2012, on 'austerity' urbanism).

In the UK, each of these areas of changes has been underpinned by a growing reduction of access to specialist legal advice, assistance and representation. While 'Access to Justice' is typically conceived in the context of criminal law, the extraordinary cuts to Civil Legal Aid introduced by the Legal Aid, Sentencing and Punishment of Offenders Act 2012 (LASPO) have made clear the critical importance of 'access to justice' in the context of, among other issues, redress in the face of government error, mitigating the power imbalances between employers and employees, and of preventative help to fend off default on household debts.

The subtitle of the book – 'Reflections on challenging times for advice agencies' – reflects our desire that this be a book not only about advice but *from* advice; we wanted the voices and opinions of clients, advisers and managers to come to the fore. In addition to weaving material from the project through the book chapters, we have included three 'case studies' – stories of individuals participating in our research that trace their encounter with advice services. We have used these as the basis for reflections on the issues at stake in the individual cases, on the processes that people encounter when they seek advice, and on the practices, possibilities and problems of advice work in 'austerity'.

How to use this book

The book is separated into three parts, each covering a different area of concern that guided the research project. Each part begins with an introductory page setting out the questions to which the grouped papers are responding and the narrative threads that link them. Unlike other texts in this field, across these three parts the reader will find a variety of writing styles and chapter formats. The book combines personal vignettes[*] with presentations of research; legal analysis with

---

[*]   All participant names used in the text are pseudonyms.

theoretical perspectives; and edited interviews with agendas for political change. It can be read from cover to cover, moving between styles and narrative threads, or across points of interest that move between chapters. Some chapters are designed to speak directly to each other. Thus the 'case studies', which present the stories of research participants as they interact with advice services, are followed by 'Reflections' in which three advice experts reflect upon what these vignettes say about their area of work. The final chapter of the book reflects upon the issues and themes raised across the different contributions, considering what they tell us about the current (and future) political situation and the role of advice in resisting dynamics of social and economic dislocation.

We hope this distinct approach provides an engaging and novel reading experience for the variety of individuals with interests in the field of advice. To give an idea of where these varied interests are addressed across the text, for readers coming into advice either as a subject or a practice, Eleanor Kirk (Chapter Five) and Samuel Kirwan (Chapter Nine) describe the experience of advice and its effects upon advisers and clients, while the contributions of Sue Evans (Reflection on Case study one) and Joe McGlade (Reflection on Case study three) provide first-hand accounts of the challenges facing advisers and the teams that support them. For readers looking for indications of how advice is changing, Jennifer Harris (Chapter Three) and John Clarke (Chapter Ten) indicate respectively the changing technological and social dynamics that shape the work of advice services; Nicole Busby (Chapter Four) and Eleanor Kirk (Chapter Five) examine the growing importance within the advice sector of employment law; and Morag McDermont (Chapter One) and Gail Bowen-Huggett (Chapter Two) analyse how funding patterns and relationships are changing. For readers looking for practical guidance on 'good' advice, Alison Kite (Chapter Seven) explores how advice work can empower clients while Emily Rose (Chapter Eight) examines effective ways in which stories are transformed into practical information. For readers looking for the broader social and legal implications of advice, Adam Sales (Chapter Six) examines how employment advice relates to the contemporary condition of 'precarity', while Michael Ford (Reflection on Case study two) argues that the problems faced by employment clients indicates a 'new normal' in which access to justice is blocked by procedural reforms. Finally, for readers wishing to understand what advice tells us about political action, Nicole Busby (Chapter Four) details the necessary changes within the Employment Tribunal (ET) context if clients from all backgrounds are to access 'justice', while John Clarke (Chapter Ten) situates a narrative of 'citizenship' as a rallying point for a politics attentive to injustices and struggles that compose contemporary society.

We hope that the book will offer readers, both within and outside the field, different perspectives on the role played by advice work, as well as a celebration of its importance and centrality to the current political situation in the face of considerable challenges. We hope it serves as a tool, a guide and an inspiration.

What is advice?

Many of our participants were quick to tell us that, contrary to received opinion, to receive advice is not to be told what to do. Several advisers emphasised instead, when describing their work, the provision of accurate and appropriate information in a language the client can understand – work oriented towards enabling clients to make informed decisions. Advice was seen as making comprehensible what was distant and unintelligible; it made possible those future actions that had been riven with foreboding and anxiety. Some questioned whether the term 'advice', with the emphasis upon directing an individual towards a certain course of action, was the right term for this work. It is important to note also that the typical advice 'journey' with the Citizens Advice service will begin with something very different again: a diagnostic interview in which no information is given at all (see Reflection on Case study one). Following this, there may be a wait before an advice appointment, as it is typically imagined, takes place.

With these considerations in mind, we continue to value the term 'advice' as a description of the provision of information and all that happens around it: the work of translating law into the everyday language of the client; the work of diagnosing and prioritising problems; the work of teasing out what the actual problems are behind what the client has been comfortable to present with; and also the institutional and procedural work of organising, funding and publicising services. We hope that across the text an image of advice that carries these complexities, whilst retaining the importance of advice both to the advisee and the adviser, is able to take shape.

Tackling 'austerity': changing times for advice

Among the many 'austerity' policies of the Coalition and Conservative governments, in this section we focus further on two particular areas that played a key role in shaping the advice field during the period of our research: cuts to legal aid and 'welfare reform'. It is important to begin, however, by noting that attempts to scale back the provision of legal aid, and the ensuing effect upon advice agencies, have been a defining feature of political approaches to 'access to justice' long before the introduction of LASPO in 2012.

Thus, when the new Labour government introduced Community Legal Service Partnerships (CLSPs) in 1999, with the idea that providers and funders of advice services would form partnerships at a local government level, their implementation was coupled to a cap on the civil legal aid budget as part of a move from a demand-led system of legal aid funding to a planned system based on local legal needs assessments. CLSPs therefore were constituted within the context of rationing of legal aid and increased competition for resources between advice providers (Moorhead, 2001: 556). Partnerships were able to raise the profile of legal advice services, and to build relationships between funders, between providers and between funders and providers. However, resource restraints often made it difficult for partnerships to move into joint strategic action (Moorhead, 2001: 558)

In 2006, the Legal Services Commission (LSC) stopped facilitating CLSPs and their attention turned instead to working with local authorities to jointly commission advice services in the form of Community Legal Advice Centres and Community Legal Advice

Networks. Again, however, the commissioning model was developed within the context of significant changes to legal aid, including making payments to providers through fixed fees rather than through hourly rates, and setting targets for the number of cases which providers had to take on. The competitive nature of the commissioning process threatened the existence of advice services; large private sector companies could come in and successfully bid, leaving the local advice agencies without funding. The process of drawing up the service specifications was also contentious; the needs assessments were criticised by advice agencies, as were the targets for client numbers, and in addition advice organisations argued that the process threatened their independence and freedom.

Nonetheless the scale of the cuts implemented through LASPO, underpinned by the replacement of the Legal Services Commission (a non-departmental public body) by the Legal Aid Agency (housed within the Ministry of Justice), represented a new era of 'late modern' or 'austerity' justice (Maclean and Eekelaar, 2016; Hynes, 2013). As Steve Hynes argues, following the 'Rose Garden' meeting between David Cameron and Nick Clegg that formed the Coalition Government in 2010, 'it had taken … just under two years … to introduce legislation to dismantle a large chunk of the civil legal aid system which had evolved since 1949 to provide access to justice for the public' (Hynes, 2013: 125).

In the intervening years it has been the cuts to criminal legal aid that have received greatest attention; following sustained criticism and legal challenge the moves to significantly cut the number of criminal practices providing duty solicitor work were shelved by the new Justice Minister Michael Gove in 2016. Yet it is civil legal aid that bore the brunt of the cuts, with family, debt, housing and other issues being subject to a near-total removal of support.[1] This has led to stark changes in the family courts; in 2014 NAPO (the Probation and Family Court Union) reported a rise since 2012 from 18% to 42% of cases in which both parties were unrepresented, parties being ten times more likely to be appearing without legal representation (NAPO, 2014). This has created, they report, severe disruptions to court time and procedure

7

and increased unjust and inappropriate decisions. The principal effects for participants in our research are, however, more diffuse and harder to measure, being shaped by the disappearance of trained legal experts able to advise individuals in these areas of civil law as independent law centres were forced to close (Mayo et al, 2014) and private solicitors were unable to provide free advice.

The second area of change affecting the demand for advice concerns the misleadingly named programme of 'welfare reform'. The potentially most wide-reaching change was the introduction of 'Universal Credit' (UC) in the Welfare Reform Act 2012, yet owing to ongoing implementation problems, UC had not yet been introduced in any of the localities in which our research took place. Nonetheless, several changes implemented by the Coalition government had significantly affected welfare entitlements. The 'under-occupancy penalty' (otherwise known as the 'bedroom tax') reduced entitlements to Housing Benefit for social housing tenants judged to have a surplus of bedrooms, creating reductions of benefit or housing displacement for many people. A 'tougher regime' of sanctions for Job Seeker's Allowance (JSA) claimants led to people who had missed an appointment being left with no money at all; while more stringent regulations and assessments, and a lengthy waiting period, for the two principal sickness and disability benefits in the UK (Employment and Support Allowance and Personal Independence Payments) caused many individuals with no capacity for work being forced into the pressures of claiming JSA. These changes were widely agreed by those participating in our research, both clients and advisers, to have created a system that is both more punitive and unfairly weighted against the most vulnerable in society. In addition to their frustrations with a system that was seen to be failing those in need, advisers noted that these problems typically created many-stranded household debt burdens, and that cases were, on average, becoming far more complex.

About the research programme

The very significant changes described above form the backdrop to the research programme that led to this book. In 2011 the European Research Council awarded a grant to fund a four-year research programme, 'New Sites of Legal Consciousness: a Case Study of UK Advice Agencies'. The rationale behind the programme, as described in the bid, was that:

advice organisations, rather than professional lawyers, are becoming key actors in legal arenas, particularly for citizens whose relationship to rights is most precarious. At a time of ever deepening inequalities, it becomes crucial to understand how institutions such as advice agencies can mediate and make possible interventions into those spaces of everyday life that become infused with law, such as workplace relations, consumer relations and caring relations. (NSLC, 2011)

The programme contained three separate but interlinked projects, two of which focused on the work of the Citizens Advice service. A number of distinguishing features led to our focus on Citizens Advice Bureaux (CAB)[2] as a significant site for research. First, as is discussed in Chapter One, as a long-established advice organisation it is a leading player in the UK advice sector with a training programme for volunteer advisers considered to provide a benchmark for other advice organisations. Secondly, as is explored in Chapter Ten, at the time of writing the funding bid it was the largest voluntary organisation that explicitly defines itself in terms of *citizens*, thus providing a rich site to investigate how horizontal conceptions of citizenship as mutuality and egalitarianism are experienced and enacted in the advice setting (see Jones, 2010; and Kirwan et al, 2016). The following sections set out the methods employed for each research project.[3]

Project 1: Citizens Advice Bureaux and employment disputes

With the decline of trades unions and the growth in small and non-unionised firms, Citizens Advice has become increasingly important as a source of advice, and sometimes representation, for people with problems at work. This project focused on the role the CABx play when faced with clients who arrive with employment disputes that are judged to be appropriate to take to an Employment Tribunal. The research was interested in how these clients pursue their dispute following their first interaction with the CAB, on how participants identify issues and make decisions as to which routes to dispute resolution they follow, whether to pursue the dispute through the Employment Tribunal, or choose other options, or take no action at all.

Researchers worked with seven Citizens Advice Bureaux in England, Scotland and Northern Ireland, following CAB clients from their first point of contact with the bureau. Once the client had agreed to take part in the research, a researcher would observe advice appointments, interview clients and keep in contact through email and phone calls. If the client's case ended up at an Employment Tribunal, the researcher would observe the Tribunal hearing. In all we followed 158 CAB clients of whom 56 submitted a claim to the Employment Tribunal.

Project 2: Homelessness, advice provision and technology

This project explored how homeless people are using technology to access advice, information and other forms of assistance, such as Job Seeker's Allowance; and how homeless people's use of technology is affected by the ways in which ICT is provided within different organisations. Research was carried out through empirical investigation at three homelessness organisations providing ICT access and advice: a drop-in day centre; a Nightstop scheme; and a drop-in centre offering IT training. Data was collected through interviews with key stakeholders, observations at the homelessness support organisations, and interviews with homeless people using these services.

Project 3: Citizens Advice Bureaux workers and volunteers, ideas of legality and citizenship

This project examined how ideas of legality and citizenship shaped Citizens Advice, in terms of daily practices of advice-giving, their training of volunteer advisers, and their approach to social policy and campaigning. A number of distinguishing features led to our focus on the CAB as a significant site for research. First, as is discussed in Chapter One, it is a long-established generic advice organisation, a leading player in the advice sector in the UK and Europe; its training programme for volunteer advisers is considered as providing a benchmark for other advice organisations in the UK. Secondly, it is the only large-scale voluntary organisation that explicitly defines itself in terms of citizens, reflected in a horizontal conception of citizenship as mutuality – advice is offered between citizens, in keeping with an ethos of egalitarianism and anonymity.

The data for this project was collected in 2014 through 42 interviews and five focus groups with advisers, managers, trainers and trainees at CAB in England and Scotland. The researcher trained as a CAB adviser, enabling participant observation of the training process as well as producing three further diaries of the interviews recorded by other trainees.

Scope of the book

While we hope this book speaks to all those with an interest in the field of advice, covering both paid and voluntary work, and national and local services, there are two limiting factors to note in this respect. The first is that most of our fieldwork was conducted with the Citizens Advice service, for reasons discussed above. Chapters One and Ten explore further the particular organisational shape and cultural specificity of the service, rooted in its own distinctive history, that mark it out from other providers in the field.

The second relates to the attention paid to particular fields of advice work (to the exclusion of others), specifically the focus upon employment advice. The choice of employment as a field of study was deliberate. In our research we wanted to understand how people related to and engaged (or did not engage) with law as part of everyday life. However, despite the fact that the term 'the law' is in common use, law does not exist as a single entity. Different areas of life are suffused by different forms of law, some formal, some less so. The field of employment relations is a highly *legalised* field, as many advisers and lawyers with whom we spoke noted. Despite the best efforts of judges to make employment law accessible to those who seek to access it, the legal framework has developed as a series of specialised and highly specific decisions issuing from decisions of employment tribunals. Given the centrality of work in people's lives, and the intensity of emotion surrounding employment troubles, employment advice, it appeared to us, opened a particular window upon how law affects people, and how individual disputes and experiences become 'legal'.

The book has ten chapters divided into three parts.

Part One explores the forces shaping the organisation and delivery of advice services. We begin with a case study of Lucy's experiences of the barriers to accessing advice, which is followed by some reflections from Sue Evans of Bristol Citizens Advice. In Chapter One, Morag McDermont examines the changing resourcing of Citizens Advice Bureaux with a particular focus on how resources affect the way advice is organised and provided. Chapter Two broadens the focus beyond Citizens Advice to a more general discussion of the pressures, problems and possibilities of advice work in one area – Bristol and Avon – through an interview with Gail Bowen-Huggett. Finally, Jenny Harris considers the implications of current moves towards the digitisation of benefit and advice services.

Part Two examines the field of employment disputes, a highly legalised area in which advice workers are making an increasingly important contribution. We begin with a case study of Laura, dismissed from her job on grounds that she, and her advisers, considered to be unfair. Ultimately, Laura could not afford to pursue her dispute through the Employment Tribunal because of the high cost of tribunal fees. In his response, employment barrister Michael Ford examines the problems of advising on unfair dismissal cases, and the dramatic impact of fees cases brought to ETs. Nicole Busby follows with an overview of key areas of employment law dealt with by CABx. Eleanor Kirk then explores the interaction between law and access to justice through the research data, focusing on two key questions: how do people think about the law in relation to disputes with their employers, and how do advisers transform these notions into action or inaction in relation to employment disputes? In the last chapter of Part Two, Adam Sales focuses on the precarious workers who formed a large proportion of the CABx clients in our research. For these workers, the intervention of CAB advisers could at times offset some of the increasing exploitation of the worker's labour.

Part Three explores some of the complex dynamics of advice work. Beginning from Brian's case, we consider how charging fees for tribunals has implications for people seeking advice, with a discussion by Joe McGlade. This raises wider issues about the 'costs of justice' that are probed in a chapter by Nicole Busby. In the following chapter Alison Kite examines the powerlessness which people can experience in their encounters with the benefits system and the ways that advice can help to address this. Then Samuel Kirwan looks at the emotional labour of advice work, considering how advisers respond to, and manage emotionally charged issues and experiences presented to them by clients.

The book concludes with a reflection on the role advice work plays in practising citizenship (exploring the citizen in Citizens Advice) and the possibilities and problems of doing such work in 'austere' times.

Notes

[1] While it was recognised that exceptional cases, including individuals facing domestic violence, remained deserving of funding, significant problems remain with regard the 'additional hurdle of exceptionality' (Cobb, 2013: 15) one must negotiate to access this support.

[2] In this book we use the term 'Citizens Advice service' to refer to the two national organisations, Citizens Advice (commonly known as CitA, which covers England Wales and the North Ireland/Northern Ireland) and Citizens Advice Scotland (CAS) and the local organisations, until recently known as 'the CAB' or Citizens Advice Bureau. CitA has recently undergone a somewhat controversial rebranding exercise, one result of which was to remove the term 'bureau', which was considered old-fashioned. However,

we have found it difficult to come up with another term which denotes the local offices of Citizens Advice, and so have maintained the usage of CAB throughout this book

[3] More details of all publications and work of the research programme are available on the project website (NSLC, 2016).

PART ONE
INTRODUCTION

John Clarke and Samuel Kirwan

Where else to start this exploration of advice work but at the front door of a service: at the long, orderly queue that forms over the hours before the service opens. Over the course of our project this queue, witnessed across multiple cities and different types of service, seemed to grow with each passing month, cementing the importance of advice providers in times of increasing inequality and social change. As the demand for advice has increased, the challenges for those organising services have become more complex and time-consuming. In an era when 'digital by default' is celebrated across public services, the model of the drop-in, and face-to-face advice, appears increasingly anachronistic: why queue for advice when the information is available online, or on the end of a phone?

These chapters examine the organisation and funding of advice services in times of increased demand, looking both at individual services and the relationships between them at the local and regional levels. They explore how organisational responses to these challenges shape the experience of advice, most notably with regard the complex considerations that inform how much attention an individual will be given on that first visit, and whether they will be given a full appointment or referred elsewhere. The chapters also engage with how changing uses of technology have affected both advice seeking and the advice being given: what does the era of 'digital by default' mean for those whose lives are indeed dominated by digital technologies, but not necessarily in the way imagined?

Part One begins with Lucy's story, articulating the barriers that stand between a citizen and the advice they seek. Lucy's experiences are explored by Sue Evans, manager of the Bristol Citizens Advice Bureau. Chapter One then locates the work of Citizens Advice in the context of austerity politics and policies, creating new pressures and problems for those providing urgently needed services. Chapter Two takes the form of an interview with Gail Bowen-Huggett exploring the problems facing the advice sector as a whole in this moment. The final chapter in this part explores the promises and limitations of digital routes to advice, assessing their likely consequences for providers and service users.

These chapters are timely - speaking to a critical moment for advice services: how have these organisations sought to survive and adapt in a period of profound social and technological change?

'LUCY': THE BARRIERS TO ACCESSING ADVICE

Case study compiled by Jennifer Harris

Lucy was 25 years old and 13 weeks pregnant when she first became homeless following the non-payment of wages from a previous employer. Lucy actively sought advice and information about her housing rights and options from 11 different sources. Within this process, Lucy encountered a number of barriers which significantly impacted on the speed and ease with which she was able to access targeted advice.

The story

In 2014 Lucy moved from Scotland to the South of England to take up a new employment position. Upon arrival she was informed by her previous employer that they had decided not to release her holiday pay. Lucy depended on this money to put down a deposit on a new flat and as a result was left homeless and in a particularly vulnerable position:

'I was pregnant, I had my suitcase, all of my belongings, I'd been carrying it around for three days now. I also have a heart condition, so I was prone to fainting, which is rubbish.'

Lucy initially approached the local authority at the main Customer Service Point (CSP) where she waited two and a half hours for an appointment. Since she lacked a connection to the local area, Lucy was turned away without an opportunity to speak to a housing options adviser. Staff at the CSP appeared unconcerned, unsympathetic and unwilling to provide even basic information:

'I didn't ask for anything, I asked for advice, even just a list of services … I didn't go in there and say, "can you get me like a two-bedroomed flat, something really nice?" I literally just wanted to know advice about what I could do, like who I could talk to that could kind of give me a hand and they're like, can't really help you cos you've got no connection … so they didn't even give me like a list of people to talk to or refer me to anybody else.'

Lucy felt that despite being a victim of unforeseen and uncontrollable circumstances, staff at the CSP appeared to assume that she had intentionally made herself homeless:

'It was sort of like as if I'd thought it would be really funny if I tried to move down with £50 in my back pocket and 13 weeks pregnant and just see what happens.'

Lucy had volunteered for a homelessness shelter in Scotland prior to becoming homeless and was therefore aware of Shelter's housing advice helpline. Lucy telephoned this helpline and was advised to visit her local Citizen's Advice Bureau (CAB). Lucy argued that as "their [Scotland's] homeless procedure is much different", this volunteering experience had not helped to her to be aware of her housing rights and options.

Lucy visited the local CAB where she attended a gateway appointment. Lucy argued that at this point, the urgency of her situation and the prospect that help might not be available contributed to heightened feelings of anxiety and emotional distress:

'They gave me like a really small slot – which I understand and appreciate because they have to see an awful lot of people. So yeah, they saw me about 5 minutes … she said you've got no connections to Bristol, there's not really a service that we think would help you.'

The gateway adviser provided Lucy with a booklet listing information on local services and general advice for homeless people. Lucy began to panic at the prospect of sleeping rough and as a result felt averse to using this particular information resource:

'There was nothing they could really do to be honest. So it was kind of a panic but they gave me a little booklet, basically of "how to be homeless" and where to sleep and all that kind of stuff. And I was, like, I don't want this, this is awful.'

Lucy was new to the local area and was therefore completely unaware of the nature and location of available services or how to go about accessing them. After leaving the CAB, Lucy tried using the computers at the local public library to find advice and information about her housing rights and options. However, lacking the local address required to obtain a library card, she was only given 15 minutes on a 'guest computer', a time period which was entirely insufficient to find the advice and information she needed. Lucy also attempted to locate services using one of the free public internet portals located throughout the city centre but was hardly surprised that this search was unsuccessful, stating that "obviously homeless provisions aren't going to be on there".

With the help of google maps on her phone and the booklet provided by CAB, Lucy eventually located a drop-in day centre catering to homeless and vulnerable people. Staff at this service advised Lucy to get a doctor's note to confirm she was pregnant in order to increase her chances of being classified as being in priority need. The doctor however refused to see Lucy because she lacked a local address. Lucy then returned to the drop-in centre where staff suggested she should go back to the doctor using them as a reference. After another long wait, the doctor still refused to see Lucy. This in turn had a particularly detrimental impact on Lucy's psychological and emotional wellbeing:

'At the doctor's – if you're pregnant, tearful and homeless, to be told, well, you haven't got an address, we can't see you, it was really really difficult.'

Lucy then approached the police for assistance, where she was provided with a telephone number for a local emergency accommodation service. This service informed Lucy that whilst "they would see what they could do", due to her lack of local connection it was unlikely that she would be able to access any emergency accommodation. This particular service then failed to return Lucy's phone call despite promising to do so.

Lucy had to walk around the city for several hours with all her belongings whilst looking for appropriate services and attending appointments. Being 13 weeks pregnant and suffering from a chronic heart condition, meant that this process proved particularly arduous and time-consuming. Lucy depended heavily on her smart phone for the purpose of navigating the city and to communicate with different services. A lack of places to charge her phone operated as a barrier, with Lucy having to limit the use of her phone in order to conserve the battery.

It was 17:45pm when Lucy left the doctors' for the second time. As this point services were closing and Lucy began to worry that she would have to spend the night sleeping rough. Lucy then remembered that the Shelter helpline had given her the telephone number of the local Nightstop scheme. Nightstop subsequently provided her with emergency accommodation, advice and support.

Reflecting on her experience, Lucy argued that services were often difficult to find and inadequately advertised. The barriers Lucy experienced in her search for advice and information led her to conceptualise advice as a scarce resource which appeared to be hidden from those lacking knowledge or experience:

'Obviously people need to help themselves but you shouldn't really have to kind of hide it from people. It's like we'll offer you services if you can find it.'

A REFLECTION ON CASE STUDY ONE: THE BARRIERS TO ACCESSING ADVICE

Sue Evans[*]

Anyone who works in the advice sector, and perhaps those in the wider public as well, know that the demand for advice outstrips supply. We know that scantly resourced services struggle to meet demand, and that economic 'austerity' has delivered a double blow to those seeking advice, stripping away much-needed services whilst also adding to the problems of the advice seekers, afflicted with poverty, worklessness, debt and homelessness.

Most of us also realise that the pressure on our services, the constant squeeze of 'more for less' reducing funding pots and increasing targets has a knock-on effect on the clients, one that is not simply a case of them having to wait longer to be seen. Our day-to-day focus, however, tends to be on what it's like for us: the service struggling to make ends meet. And whilst we would claim to understand the wider economic plight of our clients, and will speak with authority and empathy about their lives – what it's like to live on benefits, lose your job, struggle with ill health – rarely do we stop to consider practically what it might be

[*] Sue Evans is Director of Bristol Citizens Advice, and has an in-depth knowledge of advice work, having spent the last 28 years managing a variety of independent third sector and statutory advice services.

like to be a client accessing one of these overstretched under-resourced services. We ask for feedback in a mechanistic 'how was it for you' sort of a way, but it's rare for us to look in detail at how our services work for a specific set of circumstances relating to an individual.

Lucy's story brings the personal experience of the advice seeker into sharp relief. She was searching for possibly the most difficult of all things in Bristol – an affordable place to live. She was also able to demonstrate a high degree of self-sufficiency and capability, and she had a job, although the case study would suggest she had not at that point started working. It isn't possible to understand in retrospect quite how she presented to those she approached for advice, but it is likely that she came across as capable and in control, and didn't really draw very much on her actual vulnerability, her heart condition, her pregnancy, her lack of local knowledge or contacts. She probably felt that she appeared upset because she was upset, but in comparison to many people seen in advice and statutory agencies she may actually not immediately have presented as truly 'vulnerable'.

To meet demand, services are increasingly relying on prioritisation of clients by relative vulnerability, whilst at the same time debating and failing to find a consensus on what vulnerability in modern-day Bristol actually looks like. Someone presenting as able to take action for themselves will invariably be categorised at not being vulnerable and so we encourage self-help, assuming that they will be able to access the information they need. So did Lucy actually suffer a poor advice experience partly as a result of this approach? Did she present as being too capable to get the help she needed? If that is the reality, it is a terrible indictment of the sector.

Lucy's interaction with the Customer Service Point (CSP) at the Council highlights the effect that having nothing to offer has on local authorities. The public perception of the local authority being 'there for everyone' belies the reality of public services that manage the effect of major funding cuts and ration service by applying one stark and simple rule: 'do we have a statutory responsibility?' The answer of course is usually in the negative, and this can translate at a human level into 'I don't have to help you, so I won't'. Nonetheless, the overall poor experience at the CSP reflects on how far removed from an ethos of public service – of being there to help – we have become. There wouldn't really be much of a cost or a time implication in giving Lucy the type of simple leads she needed and it would have made a difference to her very early on in her search.

Her experience of a Citizens Advice 'Gateway' appointment was no more flexible or effective, with accurate but basic and ultimately unhelpful information provided. The Gateway appointment, a triaging system introduced into the service from 2010 onwards, provides a client with an initial point of contact with Citizens Advice and is designed to assess what help they need, and whether Citizens Advice can provide it, or whether other providers are better placed to help. Where there is nothing appropriate to offer the client this should be explained and in an ideal situation some lateral thinking could be introduced to try to help the client manage the situation they face.

Lucy's experience of approaching Citizens Advice highlights the basic weakness of the triage system in that it is a method of managing demand, not a method of maximising service quality. In reality it is a process put in place more for the benefit of the organisation operating it than the clients it works with. Experienced advice workers will always explain that it takes time to find out what a client really wants, to get past the initial presenting problem and get under the skin of the issue, getting a feel for the client's own values and relative capability whilst you explore what can be difficult and embarrassing information for someone to reveal to a stranger. You can't do that in the ten-minute timeframe allowed for a Gateway appointment. Lucy's view, that "They gave me like a really small slot – which I understand and appreciate because they have to see an awful lot of people", is too forgiving of a broken process. A clear demonstration of this 'brokenness' is to be seen every day in our waiting room in Bristol, where before the morning drop-in session starts, the Duty Manager for the day gives a short announcement to all the waiting clients explaining how the system works and what to expect. It's a graphic illustration of managing expectations downwards, because, in reality, that short explanation is to explain in advance to clients that they aren't going to get what they want that day, and that they will almost certainly have to come back for the actual advice they are seeking.

We are constantly looking at ways to improve the Gateway experience, and now try whenever possible to recognise when a client will benefit from 'discrete or one-off advice' - something that can happen there and then in only a little longer than the allotted ten-minute slot; a letter drafted, a phone call made, or a quick action plan of next steps can all be enormously helpful to someone who has plucked up the courage to come and ask for help. It also improves the management of demand more effectively than the provision of a set ten-minute advice slot 'come what may' inasmuch as it prevents work from being queued and gives the clients a better service.

The theme of statutory services only helping where they had a duty to do so persists throughout Lucy's story as the police and doctors also failed to help her (although it seems perverse that a medical service would fail to offer at least some support to a pregnant woman with a chronic medical condition). That Lucy found 'Nightstop' was more by luck and her own research than through the help of any agency in the city; it is probably the only place that she could have ended up in the very short term. However, getting to that point was unnecessarily arduous. All Lucy actually needed was time, somewhere to stop and work through her problem and where she could access local information and check her assumptions with someone who knew the local area. The places Lucy approached were all sensible, logical choices, and ideally the library could or maybe should have been a source of the information needed. Once local connections wouldn't have been an issue when using a library to access reference material, and details of local services would have been available in hard copy or microfiche which anyone could browse to their heart's content. Today nearly all such information is web-based and can only be reached if you have access to the equipment needed. The drive towards digital inclusion focuses very much on personal ability to use the internet, but IT skills are useless if you can't actually get hold of a computer to use.

From my perspective, the case study leaves me wondering how we could be more adaptable in the scope of additional services we offer. I would like to think that we could develop our existing public access IT to give clients the ability to research across a wider range of resources, as at present our system is 'locked down' to a few specific sites – the Council, DWP, Money Advice Service principally – to protect the integrity of our systems and ensure that our public access area is not misused; however, you can see the limitations in this approach that could in reality prevent people like Lucy from accessing the information they need. Possibly we should also look at the feasibility of holding a range of local information in hard copy – an approach that in the era of the internet is often seen as outmoded and unnecessary – but giving Lucy information of this type, somewhere to sit and read it and a plug to enable her to charge her phone would probably have been all that was needed to put her on the right track much earlier in the day. Whether this type of flexibility is realistic is something to be discussed, yet as I touched on earlier in relation to the Gateway service, the question remains that of whether we are running the service in a way that really helps people, or rather just designing in checks and balances that make our lives easier. Turning to the values of the service, we say that Citizens Advice gives people 'the help they need for the problems they face', a principle we need to keep in mind at all times.

The study also illustrates the experience of being a stranger in Bristol. We see 'our' city as welcoming and well supplied with sources of advice and information. We 'know' what's out there and where to find it, almost subconsciously. Few of us will have stopped to consider whether someone new to the area can find the services we all know so well, and this case study hasn't even touched on the additional issues many newly arrived people will experience, namely those of not speaking English and having little understanding of our culture and how the UK works. The difficulties Lucy faced should be noted when we develop and advertise our services and train our staff and volunteers, as surely in the City of Sanctuary it should be possible for newly arrived people to get the help and information they need without having to struggle to find it.

1

CITIZENS ADVICE IN AUSTERE TIMES

Morag McDermont[*]

Introduction

Lucy's story of trying to access advice in Bristol, and Sue Evans' response on the ever-increasing and conflicting stresses and strains of advice, give a rich indication of the constantly shifting challenges facing advice seekers and those attempting to deliver advice services. In this chapter I examine the history, funding and regulatory environment of Citizens Advice, the largest voluntary sector advice organisation in the UK and the principal subject of our research programme. The structure of Citizens Advice – national umbrella organisations providing services, support and guidance to local autonomous charitable organisations that themselves rely heavily on a volunteer workforce – is both unique and critically important to the strength and adaptability of the service. Advice work forms the first 'pillar' of the service, while the national/

[*]   Morag McDermont is Professor of Socio-Legal Studies in the University of Bristol. In 2011 she was awarded a research grant by the European Research Council for 'New Sites of Legal Consciousness: a case study of UK advice agencies'. Morag has previously worked in local government and the housing association sector.

local structure also enables the service to deliver its second 'pillar': using the intelligence from its advice-giving work to influence social policy.

In this chapter, I will focus on the ways in which the resourcing of the service has been changing, concentrating on three key forms of resource and support: the relationships between national and local organisations; the funding of bureaux; and the volunteer workers in advice. Each of these elements is changing in ways that have profound implications for the provision of advice and point to an increasingly unsettled future. I conclude with an assessment of the threats and further challenges to this voluntary sector advice service.

Citizens Advice: an overview

The Citizens Advice service is comprised of a network of local associations, each being, until recently, known as a 'Citizens Advice Bureau' or 'CAB', connected to and supported by the national bodies Citizens Advice and Citizens Advice Scotland. Citizens Advice Bureaux were first established in 1939, in part as a response to the anticipated disorders and dislocations of citizens facing war (Figure 1.1). The idea of a voluntary advice service had first been raised alongside reforms of the Public Assistance system in 1924 in the report of the Betterton Committee on Public Assistance Administration. The original bureaux, of which the image of the bureau located in a horse-box (Figure 1.2) that would travel to bomb-damaged areas has become symbolic, were committed to this voluntary principle and were supported by funds from local councils.

As the war continued the service grew considerably: by 1942 over 1000 bureaux were operating around the UK. Despite increased demand for advice in the post-war welfare state, the service retracted to 416 in 1960. In the 1970s the service underwent a significant expansion linked to the nascent consumer movement and increased governmental support for the provision of consumer advice. Following a large grant from the Ministry of Trade and Consumer Affairs, the number of bureaux rose to 566 in 1973 and then 818 by 1978-79 (Citron, 1989: 3).

Figure 1.1: Public information posters, 1939

© Citizens Advice

Local Citizens Advice Bureaux are separately registered charities, each with its own management structure and board of trustees. In many towns they have become part of the network of local services: town centre signage will provide direction to the CAB (Figure 1.3); Council tax bills often direct people to the local CAB if they are having trouble with payments. Such recognition of the importance of the local CAB has meant that (as discussed further below), until recently they have largely been funded by a grant from the local council.

However, particularly since the election of the Coalition government in 2010, CABx have become enmeshed in the turbulent landscape of shifting organisational, legislative and regulatory arrangements for the delivery of a 'public service' of advice described in the Introduction to this book. Most recently the terrain has been characterised by shifting and intensifying patterns of social need, particularly in the period of the politics and policies of 'austerity'. Cuts in funding both to local government and Civil Legal Aid have placed an increasing emphasis on voluntary or not-for-profit service provision, whilst at the same time expecting this sector to become more 'professionalised', driven to meet 'targets' and outcomes of funders. For Citizens Advice one impact of this has been an ongoing period of mergers, consolidations and closures of local offices, accompanied by an expansion of the sites through which advice is delivered. At the time of writing there are 338 bureaux operating from 3300 locations in England and Wales, 28 in Northern Ireland and 61 in Scotland (Citizens Advice, 2016; Citizens Advice Scotland, 2016). There are also pressures to move away from the face-to-face provision of advice towards telephone and digital provision, both of which change the relationship between local bureaux and the national organisations.

There are two fundamental aspects of the service, running through this history into the present, that it is important to highlight in light of these challenges. The first, the *holistic* approach to advice was identified in our interviews with CAB staff and volunteers: advisers recognise that the problem presented by a client at their first interview is usually one of many, and are trained to deal with all forms of problem.

The second is the interrelationship between the delivery of an advice service at the local level and the principle of intervention in social policy issues, where evidence from the problems brought into local offices are used to identify the need for change.[1] This leads to a commitment to 'campaign for policy changes that benefit the population as a whole' (Citizens Advice, 2016); and to 'work for a fairer Scotland where people are empowered and their rights respected' (Citizens Advice Scotland, 2016). However, as discussed in the conclusion, this second pillar to the Citizens Advice service is under threat from recent government policy changes.

National organisations as resource and as regulation

Local bureaux are autonomous organisations that are members of the national associations, namely Citizens Advice (CitA), Citizens Advice Scotland (CAS) and Citizens Advice Northern Ireland (CANi). The role of the national organisations can loosely be divided into three elements: providing support and resources; setting and maintaining standards; and social policy translation. The relationship between local and national is complex, changing and different geographically, but it is a relationship that is not simply about supporting local services but also shapes and constrains the local delivery of advice in important ways.

Figure 1.2: A CAB in the 1940s

© Citizens Advice

The training of volunteers as generalist advisers is delivered at a local level through resources and materials provided by CitA, CAS and CANi. Specialist advice training is also provided by the national organisations as well as external agencies. The national organisations are further involved in constructing what counts as 'good advice' through the public-facing online resource *AdviceGuide* (now simply CitizensAdvice.org.uk), and the internal information system *AdviserNet*, accessible only to advisers and discussed further in Chapter Nine.

The training programme and advice guides are not simply resources, but mechanisms which can shape relationships and practices. Through the public-facing site Citizens Advice is not only making a statement about the organisation's position as expert advice provider; through remodelling the service they have been able to shape it to become primarily a self-help tool as part of shifting the giving of advice away from face-to-face towards digital provision. There is a clear intention to place Citizens Advice as a leader in this, as articulated by Beatrice Karol Burke, Chief Digital Officer with CitA:

> Citizens Advice [website] currently hosts myriad topics that give advice on what something is and tries to cover every angle – despite there being little or no evidence that we need to do so.
>
> As a charity competing in a saturated marketplace, we now need to be ruthless in focusing on the core proposition of the organisation: *we help people to solve a problem.*
>
> We don't need to tell people what something is – they wouldn't be coming to us if they didn't know it affects them – we need to tell them what they can do with their current circumstance. (Karol Burks, 2015)

Figure 1.3: CABx have become part of the local townscape

© Samuel Kirwan

A more obvious way in which the national organisations shape and constrain local bureaux is through the process of regular audit of advice casework. In interviews bureaux managers were largely positive about this process, mainly as a mechanism for showing funders the quality of the service, and as a mechanism for 'passporting' through external funders' auditing processes. Indeed, many Scottish bureaux are choosing to sign up to another set of standards: National Standards in Advice.

One manager described the present Citizens Advice audit as 'heavy touch', a system that provides a decision as to whether the bureau needs auditing again next year or in three years' time. He described the *more modern pilot* which his office had signed up to "which is us regularly reviewing case records and then sending our findings to CA who independently check them" – in effect a system which requires bureaux to self-audit.

The audit explosion in the 1980s resulted in significant academic research around the impact of a climate where audit has become ubiquitous (for example, Power, 1997). As organisations change to ensure they comply with auditors' requirements, questions need to be asked about the expertise of auditors that is shaping organisations. One interviewee suggested that, in moving to the Gateway triage system (as discussed by Sue Evans earlier), it was the auditors who were holding back a change in the ways bureaux could work, maintaining older imaginings of the aims and outcomes of advice.

A further resource provided and maintained centrally is the electronic system for recording client enquiries, an entry for each client by name, basic demographic data, details of the client enquiry(s) and actions taken by the adviser and the relevant social policy codes. One purpose of the database system is to enable information to be shared across the service; it enables not only different advisers within bureaux to see the same client but also for advisers in other bureaux to do the same.

The client recording system also enables Citizens Advice to draw upon data from the several million clients they see annually to identify changing trends in the advice needs of the population and launch policy campaigns based upon them. The data provides unique and unrivalled evidence of shifting societal needs, data that is particularly powerful in a climate that puts considerable weight on evidence backed up by big numbers. Again, it should be noted that it is Citizens Advice that ultimately directs and shape these campaigns, a role that has been placed under particular scrutiny following recent government changes to funding contracts designed to limit the voluntary sector's ability to 'lobby' (discussed further below).

Funding advice work

Citizens Advice Bureaux at the local level have historically received the majority of their funding through a local authority grant. This picture has now changed dramatically. A manager of one bureau explained that they now received grants from the two separate local authorities, issue-specific grants from the Primary Care Trust and the Money Advice Service, two further sources of outreach funding (one from Sure Start) and a recent grant from the RAF Benevolent Fund. The rest, she explained "comes through donations from parish councils, town council, our own fundraising efforts and then mainly applying for small grants".

Thus most CAB budgets now look more like a mosaic, made up from a diverse range of funding sources: statutory, charitable and business. Indeed, as another bureau director explained: "we have a principle of trying to retain as diverse a funding base as we can. Survival seems to depend on that these days".

Changes in funding shifts the role of CAB managers. To survive, organisations have to become 'entrepreneurial', skilled at spotting opportunities and selling the service to potential funders. What a bureau can do – and the people it can serve – becomes increasingly dependent on what funding can be found and the partnerships and relationships developed (see Chapter Two). Our interviews revealed the extent to which services have become more project-based and funding becomes a matter of competition. Relationships with local councils change not only because funding levels are cut; the move from grants to commissioning and increasingly to competitive tendering, shifts the ways bureaux can evolve.

Clearly funding acts as an enabler, providing resources to employ staff or train volunteers to deliver advice services. But the funding source also regulates: funding sources targeted towards specific actions, goals or populations allow advice to be delivered in new ways or to a previously neglected client group, but at the same time require the organisation to direct resources to these tasks and away from others. In the process, the holistic approach to advice is placed in question by funding which comes tied to specifically identified needs.

Another anxiety expressed concerning funding was around independence. One adviser described how he sometimes felt that they are sometimes put in a 'very difficult position' by their funders:

> 'sometimes I'm being put in a position of some sort of proxy rent collector for the Local Authority ... particularly if the follow-up from the initial appointment is the Housing Officer badgering me by email or telephone: "oh, they've not paid their rent this week". And I'm thinking, that is not my job, that's your job. I've advised them about what they can do. I'm implementing the strategy that we've agreed. If the tenant is still not choosing to pay their rent, then that is their choice and they know the consequences.'

Here the adviser indicates the ways in which funding can not only dictate where and what advice is given, but also *how* it is given and for what purposes.

Like other voluntary sector advice organisations, some, but by no means all, Citizens Advice Bureaux received legal aid funding through contracts from the Legal Services Commission. This enabled them to provide specialist legal support in a variety of fields: employment, housing, welfare benefits. The drastic cuts in the legal aid budget brought in by the Coalition government in 2012 have had a major impact on CAB: for those directly funded, it has meant cutting a service (sometimes replaced by volunteers); those bureaux not affected by loss of funding have nevertheless experienced increasing demand as other services funded by legal aid were closed down.

Volunteers as resource

A third and vital element of the resourcing of advice work in CABx involves the volunteer workforce. The volunteers make up the majority of the front-line generalist advisers with the service and are also central to the peer-to-peer ethos of Citizens Advice. In return, considerable resources are put into creating and maintaining this volunteer workforce. It takes nine months to turn a new volunteer into an adviser: an extensive (usually six-month) training programme and then a period of observation before being allowed to take on casework. Volunteers are supported by salaried, specialist advisers who oversee the volunteer's handling of cases in the 'backroom' of the CAB.

The volunteers certainly enable Citizens Advice to deliver more advice for less money. Bureaux may choose to find more volunteers rather than funding, as here when the manager of a Scottish bureau was asked whether she was considering applying for charitable funding:

'Probably not in the near future. I think for us managing of welfare reform is our top priority and we're looking at managing our core service to deal with that, hence the increase that's necessary in volunteers.'

Like many other voluntary organisations, Citizens Advice has experienced pressures towards greater professionalisation and managerialisation. This has led to an increasing focus upon advisers, most of whom are volunteers, as a resource that must be managed and directed. Yet inasmuch as they give their services voluntarily, and not through any form of employment contract (the 'contract' is relational: volunteers need to want to do the work), they can be a difficult resource to direct. Thus managing through a culture of imposed targets or even constrained ways of working becomes particularly challenging. A change in role, or in the demands placed upon them, or in the way the bureau is run, may not fit with their understanding of volunteering. One manager in our study talked of how 'we lost a lot of good people' when the Gateway triage system was introduced. Volunteers can choose to withdraw their 'labour', or simply not follow directions: performance management of a volunteer workforce is a particularly difficult task.

So, like the resources of national support and funding sources, volunteers can be a two-edged benefit – making advice work possible but also establishing problems and challenges. Delivering on the 'relational contract' with volunteers implies that but they must also be *cared for* by bureaux. The manager of one bureau dealing with the impact on clients of so-called 'welfare reform' and the 'bedroom tax' described how he had joined forces with Oxfam and others to set up a food share. He knew that his advisers, faced with clients whose benefits have been cut, often found themselves only able to advise: 'that's the law'. Being able to offer food share vouchers might be the only hope they felt they could provide: the vouchers acted as an offer of something to clients and motivation for advisers to keep going.

Fragile futures

In all our research with Citizens Advice we became increasingly impressed by two factors: first, the incredible *commitment* on the part of all those who worked for the service, despite the myriad changes, difficulties, frustrations and anger they face on a daily basis; but second, the *fragility* of this service that has been assembled over the decades, creating something which appears to be an iconic British institution, but which could, more or less easily, come apart.

The threats are myriad, but all have some connection to funding. Under the pressure to do more with less, one threat arises from the increasing emphasis on phone-based and digital advice, leading to a move away from the face-to-face, one-to-one relationship between adviser and client. The threat here is to the holistic ethos of the advice service, which was seen by almost all we interviewed as being central to the Citizens Advice approach. An understanding that the role of the adviser, in the first instance, was to *listen* to the person in front of them, a listening which would often mean that the problem or concern that was presented as *the* problem by the client most frequently came to be seen as one of many; that the threat of eviction arose from a history of debt which had arisen from a dismissal from work that perhaps could and should be challenged. Government officers at all levels place an increasing faith in the digital as *the* solution; in relation to advice services, most advisers would advise against this move.

A second threat is to the social policy campaigning function of Citizens Advice. From 1 May 2016 a new clause is inserted into all new or renewed central government grant agreements preventing these funds from being used to lobby or attempt to influence parliament, local government or political parties (Cabinet Office, 2016). The new clause has been condemned by charity organisations and some MPs as threatening the ability of voluntary organisations 'to bring real-world experience of service users and evidence-based expertise into the public policy debate' (Cooney, 2016) – just the sort of translation work that Citizens Advice and others have been doing using their extensive casework database.

The third threat also arises from the ideology of the present Conservative government (and its Coalition predecessor), in its unrelenting dismantling of funding for local government.[2] For whilst most of those we interviewed saw local government funding becoming less important in actual volume terms, they all identified the crucial importance of what they called 'core' local authority funding. This in effect supported the 'heart' of the organisation, paying for office space, administration, directors and other 'backroom' support. Without this funding it would not be possible to bid for the project-driven funding from charitable, statutory and private sources because there would be no one funded to do this entrepreneurial work, and there would be no premises from where the advisers – voluntary and paid – could deliver the services. Perhaps more importantly, it is this funding, typically the only funding not tied to a particular problem area or client group, that guarantees that bureaux can provide generalist advice.

Many who operate outside the voluntary sector seem to share a strange faith that the voluntary sector is strong, and can survive no matter what – that voluntary sector organisations exist because of the voluntary effort. In relation to Citizens Advice, whilst all our research points to the central importance of the voluntary effort, what we have presented here and in the rest of this book points to the interrelatedness of the voluntary resource and the public funding resource. The institution that is the advice service is a fragile, Heath Robinson-like structure: take one key element away and the whole device could crumble, collapse or melt away.

Notes

1 See Jones (2010) for a discussion of how this social policy work enables the state to understand its citizens and the impacts of its policies upon them.

2 One Chief Executive Officer of a large bureau told us that his local authority was drawing up two lists of the services: one of those they had a statutory responsibility to provide, the other where there was no responsibility through legislation. The council was considering only funding those on the first.

THE ADVICE CONUNDRUM: HOW TO SATISFY THE COMPETING DEMANDS OF CLIENTS AND FUNDERS. AN INTERVIEW WITH GAIL BOWEN-HUGGETT

Gail Bowen-Huggett and Samuel Kirwan

This chapter presents an edited interview with Gail Bowen-Huggett, Advice Development Coordinator for ACFA: The Advice Network (formerly Advice Services for Avon). Gail had a background in the commercial sector before becoming in 2004 a manager at Bristol Debt Advice Centre (now Talking Money). Following this she became involved with ACFA, managing the network as it led a series of projects between 2013 and 2016 funded by the Advice Services Transition Fund (ASTF).

The interview provides an overview of a period in which the advice sector has been subject to significant changes and faced multiple challenges. Gail observes the effect of the loss of Legal Services

Commission contracts and the role the ASTF played in mitigating this loss, questioning the capacity of the fund to create the changes it envisaged. From her experience of working with multiple agencies, she reflects upon the challenges faced by organisations with diverse funding arrangements, organisational structures and community needs. She argues in this respect for the importance of respecting the difference between paid staff and volunteers, thus highlighting a theme explored in John Clarke's chapter (Ten), namely the unique nature of the reliance upon volunteer advisers within the Citizens Advice service. Despite these differences, Gail emphasises a theme discussed in Part Three of this book, namely the central importance of face-to-face advice, and the dangerous implications of an assumption that it can be abandoned.

Interview: Samuel Kirwan and Gail Bowen-Huggett

SK: In the context of the cuts we have seen to the funding of advice agencies, I'll start by asking what the key challenges are in *managing* funding contracts.

GB: One big thing with funders is *no double-counting*. You can't double-count clients, so you have to find a way of working with funders to make them understand that the first two-and-a-half or three hours of work that you're doing with somebody is funded under this contract, but then they need further support, and that can't be funded under this contract. It becomes a hugely bureaucratic and heavy managerial task to keep track of this. And you can't have the advisers doing it because they're there to deliver advice. That's where their specialist skills are. They don't care who's funding them to do a piece of work. They have somebody in front of them, who has problems, who they want to help.

But organisations don't have that tier of middle management to do that because it's not funded. Most funding applications are looking for services, service provision, not management of the contract. So again you have that whole juggling act going on. So that was what I spent a lot of time doing and we did that very efficiently in the end at BDAC (Bristol Debt Advice Centre - now Talking Money), and were managing multiple contracts in a way that was satisfactory and bringing in external pieces of funding to help support and bolster our core services.

But all of that takes more and more resources to feed it, so you're almost developing an animal that has to be fed constantly with new ideas and new clients. So you're forced to expand services and put more pressure on your existing advisers when in fact what you should be doing is spending the time, taking the time, to work with your client groups and understand what they need. But it all becomes about feeding the funders and bringing the money in. So it's all the wrong way round.

I think it still is, although I think now agencies are starting to understand that actually you can't keep going on like that. It's got to be different. And also the problems with that system are that it's the person who turns up on the doorstep and shouts the loudest who gets the services. And what the advice sector is about is helping people who are most vulnerable. Well, those people who are most vulnerable probably can't get to your premises, so they can't access your services in that way. And that's something, again, that I think we're just starting to come to terms with and starting to think about.

SK: Tell me about ACFA.

GB: I became involved with ACFA, which is a membership body of about 40 organisations of different sizes that all provide free advice at the point of delivery to clients. The idea is to share information, develop partnership working, share resources, get together and discuss issues, and work effectively on social policy issues. So, we try and spot trends, spot common problems that clients are facing, and raise them, establishing relationships with the local authorities and national agendas to get our point of view across.

It's worked very well over the years. As a result, there's a very close connection with Bristol City Council. ACFA representatives sit on the joint planning board so they can feed directly concerns about issues while decisions are being made about where funding is going to be spent and where resources are going to be put. And so I've been doing that and I still do that.

And then in the interim I've just finished a two-year contract on the Advice Services Transition Fund project (ASTF), which came about following the massive cuts to legal aid that occurred. The six agencies, or six agencies in Bristol who received legal aid funding lost £1.5 million of funding in a year, which is a massive amount of funding to lose, and it is a testament to them that they maintain the services and are still here.

So the government after doing that suddenly thought, "Actually, that might be quite tricky for people to manage so we'll put together some funding for people to manage that transition". My personal feeling about that is that they wasted an opportunity there. I think they were so busy thinking that we can send this money out, it's a bit of a sop, I don't think that they really made people who are putting the bids in think carefully about how it was going to work in practice, what they were going to do, and, more importantly, after the two-year funding was finished, how they were going to keep those initiatives going without continued funding.

SK: What did the ASTF funding mean to ACFA?

GB: The ASTF project was designed to give advice agencies a chance to become sustainable. That was the big word – sustainable. It was all about sustainability. But what does that mean in terms of a service that you're providing for free to people in need? How is that ever going to be sustainable? The only way to make that sustainable is to start charging people for it. But then you get into the whole debate of how do you pick and choose, who pays for a service and who doesn't pay for a service? If some people are paying for a service, do they get the same level of service as the people who aren't paying for a service? It just opens up a whole minefield of issues. One of the discussions that I always hear is, "Well, what things have we got that we can sell? We have expertise. We can sell training." Well, you know, only so many people can sell training and there are already training organisations out there.

SK: How do you see the different roles played by voluntary and paid staff within advice services?

GB: I think the problem is that the government has not fully understood what advice agencies do, and it's about giving access to legal advice which they can't afford to get anywhere else. And it's not about being able to staff it by volunteers. Yes, you can have volunteers in to help people fill forms and things but you can't have volunteers delivering advice – *legal* advice. Just welfare benefits alone, the changes that have taken place in the number and type of benefits, you can't expect volunteers to be up to date on that. That's just not going to happen.

Plus, volunteers don't have to turn up for work. Whereas advisers that you're paying do. And if you want to run a service you have to *know*. You have to have people there to deliver advice when people come in through the door. So volunteers are lovely and I'm a volunteer myself and I take it very seriously, but I don't have the same attitude to things that I volunteer for as I do when I'm being paid to do them. There is a difference there. Plus, volunteering has been held up as a way to get people back into employability. Well, that's great but then that means you spent all that time training your volunteer up to do this work and work with your clients and know the basics of how to fill in these forms and support people, and great you've skilled them up, then they go and get a job and you have to start again with the next person. Well, that's a big overhead for an agency to have to carry all the time.

Because other points of contact know that services are being cut, they're trying to do more as well. And I think there is a danger regarding the line between advice and legal advice. A lot of support workers and care workers may have some basic benefits knowledge or debt knowledge, and they're handing that information on to their clients, but they're not trained advisers and they don't think that they're giving *advice* necessarily. But actually they *are* giving advice and there are certain standards and guidelines that need to be in place to give that advice because it's legal advice. They are giving legal advice and I think that potentially is a big problem, moving forward.

Plus, it's not their job. They're there to support and provide emotional support and physical support and not give that sort of advice. They don't have the skills; they don't have the fast-track contacts. Advice services know people in that department. They can make a call. They know the terminology to use, they know what will get somebody classed as a vulnerable client. They know what the rules and regulations are.

A support worker doesn't necessarily know that so even if they do take that on and try and help, it's going to take them two or three times as long to sort that problems as a trained adviser. That's not an efficient use of time. So it's about joining all of that up, and that's where I think things like ACFA are so important. But it has to be an organisation that's funded and resourced and knows what it's doing. And there's no funding out there for that.

SK: I know that in other cities the move has been towards consolidating services.

GB: Yeah, there's the hub-and-spoke model with everybody combining together into a central hub and then perhaps doing outreach services in various venues around cities, and there has been pressure from certainly Bristol City Council on the funded agencies to keep looking at that, because they see efficiencies of scale in terms of being one premises, one set of managers, maybe fewer staff. But actually we've spent a lot of time giving them information as to why that actually is a false economy, because if you brought all those services into the centre, you would lose that immediacy of contact, that understanding of your neighbourhood; you end up doing outreaches so you have an intermittent presence in the area. Well, if you're there one morning a week, how much service are you going to provide to that community within that period of time? You're not.

The other argument for consolidation is saving money on overheads – stationery, premises and so forth, but actually if you sit down and look through the finances for each of these advice agencies, they run so lean that the money goes on staff. So you'd be cutting staff, and when I say staff I mean advisers. So the only way you'd save money by consolidating is by having fewer advisers, which means you're operating a smaller service. So where's the gain?

Now, the plus sides of having individual agencies is (A) you have greater coverage, (B) you have a wider network from which to draw in volunteers to help organisations with various bits and pieces, and (C) you have a wider group of organisations that can bring in and leverage additional funding into the city. I think it's about providing the services that are required for the specific location and the specific clients. And for Bristol you need diverse agencies.

Going back to what I said about partnership working. Now, if we had true partnership working in effect, you would be able to say no matter which point of entry somebody attended for housing advice they would be sent to the most appropriate person. And that would be the most appropriate agency not only for them but in terms of funding for that agency. That doesn't happen. It's luck of the draw because, for example, say somebody comes to one of the local, non-specialist advice agencies, potentially they're legally aidable so they could refer them out, but they've got their own numbers to hit, so they're going to keep that client because they're going to want that person for the numbers for their own monitoring. And this is where we come back to funding requirements interfering with service provision, because, of course, if they don't hit their numbers they won't get the funding; that service won't be there at all. But then would it take the local agency longer to resolve that housing issue and will they be able to resolve it as efficiently as Shelter or the Law Centre?

SK: How else do you see that advice provision has changed over time?

GB: Advisers spend less time with clients now. It is more of a conveyor belt, partly due to the demand. So in order to deal with the demand you have to spend less time with each client so that you can move on to the next person. But also because year on year, funders want more and more people seen. Agencies haven't got any bigger.

Yes, there were inefficiencies in the beginning, but as each year goes by they're pared down more and more. And the other thing that I think gets forgotten about is that it takes a lot for somebody to actually come in to agencies. This whole media thing about benefit scroungers and debt being run up because people are being profligate with their credit cards and just stupid, that's not the clients that our agencies are seeing. Now, they may not be seeing the truly, truly vulnerable but they are seeing a section of society who cannot make ends meet. So they cannot get out of that poverty trap. So it is a temporary solution, a temporary respite and they are going to be back because, once again, what's causing them to get into trouble in the first place has not changed, so that has to be addressed.

Very often, when you have an adviser sitting with a client, they may have come in with, I don't know, a bailiff notice, or a letter that's threatening them with eviction, and that might be why they're there. But if the adviser is able to spend a bit of time with them talking about it, very often there will be many other issues behind it. That could be the last straw that actually forced them to come in to the agency, but there will be a lot of other problems.

If you don't have that time to spend to uncover those problems then, yes, you can deal with the issues, stop the evictions, send them on their way, but they're still damaged. Their life is still in need of help and support that will make a difference to them, and I think it's a tricky relationship between advisers and clients because a bond of trust is established, and very often once one piece of information's come out a whole load of other issues will come out which are not necessarily related to the legal issue on the table. It can be to do with mental health issues; I know advisers who've had people suddenly pouring out issues about rape and physical and mental abuse, which is not something that you can just say: "Well, I'm just here to help you with your eviction notice, I'm sorry. I'll refer you on." How can you do that when you're sitting opposite somebody who is in pain and has found the courage to give you that information?

But by the same token, that's a lot to ask an adviser to take onboard. You're taking onboard a lot of information that's horrendous sometimes, and where does that go? You don't have time because ... you come out of your client interview, you write it up, put it onto the system so that all the information is monitored, you then deal with the actual physical issue, you've probably got another client waiting, so you go in and deal with that client. Where do you offload and process all that information? And what we're seeing, of course, is more and more advisers burning out because you can't keep giving that level of support and not venting.

And I think, when you're sitting in government working out where you're going to save your few million, that the equation, and the current drive towards everything being digital or telephone or Skype seems to endorse this. Yes, there's a place for that, don't get me wrong, there is definitely a place for that.

But that's not the only solution. You can't beat face-to-face advice. And it has to be funded somehow.

SK: Thank you Gail.

THE SHIFT TO DIGITAL ADVICE AND BENEFIT SERVICES: IMPLICATIONS FOR ADVICE PROVIDERS AND THEIR CLIENTS

Jennifer Harris*

Introduction

Policy reform and funding allocations are currently directing advice provision away from face-to-face assistance and towards telephone and digital services. The shift towards digital channels has also assumed centre stage within the introduction of Universal Credit, which requires all claims to be applied for and managed via an online account.

*   Jennifer Harris started her PhD at the University of Bristol in 2012 and is also employed as a researcher at Caring in Bristol. Based at three different homelessness support organisations, Jennifer's PhD research explored how homeless people are using technology to access resources within the context of the current shift to digital advice and welfare benefit provision. Jennifer's interest in this field stems from her previous employment in various related fields, namely as a housing officer, a researcher on a hidden homelessness project, a Gateway Assessor at a Citizens Advice Bureau, and as a regular volunteer at a Christmas Shelter.

In this chapter I introduce this 'digitisation' of advice and welfare benefits as one of the key challenges the advice sector is currently facing. Drawing on interviews carried out with homeless people and the staff that support them, I explore the implications of these changes for both advice providers and their clients.

Policy context

Effective from April 2013, the Legal Aid, Sentencing and Punishment of Offenders Act 2012 (LASPO), significantly limited the availability of face-to-face advice and introduced the single mandatory Civil Legal Advice Gateway (the Gateway) for advice funded through legal aid. Under these new measures, rather than having the option of initially meeting an adviser face-to-face, people applying for legal aid must first be assessed by a telephone operator from the Civil Legal Advice service. Apart from a few exemptions,[1] the Gateway is now the only route through which people can access legal advice on the topics of debt, discrimination and special educational needs. Following an initial review, the government intends the Gateway to be expanded to almost all other areas of civil law.

The Gateway is driven primarily by financial motivations, with telephone advice thought to be less time-consuming and therefore cheaper than face-to-face advice. In addition, since telephone advice is considered to facilitate quicker and easier access to advice services than scheduled appointments, it is thought to be of equal quality or even preferable to face-to-face advice.

Advice providers are facing increased pressure to develop alternative methods of providing advice. For example, the Advice Service Transition Fund is a Big Lottery programme which, in 2013-14, awarded £67 million to not-for-profit advice providers to help them adapt to some of the funding cuts outlined in Chapter One. Central government contributed half of the funding, with preference awarded to applicants who show a commitment to transforming services according to certain core principles, which includes the development and expansion of telephone and digital services (Cabinet Office,

2012). The reduction in the availability of face-to-face advice, as associated with the cuts to legal aid, is also likely to increase the need for alternative ways of providing advice. There is, however, currently very little known about the receptivity, deterrents and successes of different channels of advice provision. Advice providers therefore have limited evidence which can be drawn upon to inform the development of these services.

Providing advice via remote channels is not a new practice. Many advice organisations have in recent years been developing alternative ways of providing advice, such as by email, telephone or web-chat services. However, making telephone advice compulsory is a novel development and is reasoned by Elizabeth O'Hara (Shelter) to illustrate how political preference and funding provisions are increasingly steering advice away from face-to-face assistance (O'Hara, 2012).

In addition to developing new ways of providing advice in the context of limited research and resources, many services now also face the challenge of helping clients adapt to an increasingly digitised welfare benefit system. Introduced in April 2013 and followed by an ongoing gradual national roll-out, Universal Credit combines a number of working-age benefits into one single payment. Universal Credit replaces channels previously in place for the application and management of benefit claims, such as the telephone and on paper – which included the option of face-to-face assistance via Job Centre Plus (JCP) or Local Authority (LA) customer service points. As part of the conditionality requirements attached to Job Seeker's Allowance (JSA), since 2013 JCP advisers can also require JSA claimants to search and apply for jobs via the website 'Universal Jobmatch'. The shift towards a self-service digital claims process marks a significant change in the way in which benefits are delivered in the UK.

Key areas of concern

There is currently very little independent research comparing different channels of advice provision. As a result, there is little evidence to support the claim that telephone advice is necessarily more effective and efficient than face-to-face provision. The Law Society has argued that, as a result, the introduction of the Gateway is based on a number of 'unsubstantiated assumptions' and is not 'evidence-based policy making' (The Law Society, 2011).

A study by Balmer and colleagues (2012) currently offers one of the only available comparisons between telephone-based and face-to-face advice. The findings from their research suggest that the characteristics of the advice seeker (age, ethnicity and gender), as well as case-relevant factors (such as how outcomes are defined and the specific issue faced by client), must all be taken into consideration when assessing the effectiveness and efficiency of remote channels of advice provision. Each of these factors will impact on the likelihood that a person will access telephone advice, the total time the advice takes and the outcomes which are achieved. For example, their study suggests that whilst telephone advice may be readily accessed for landlord/tenant issues, it will often not be accessed for issues relating to homelessness. Homelessness or threat of homeless was also found to require more time than any other case.

Other research has shown that people with more immediate problems and those with more complex needs tend to resort to face-to-face advice (Buck et al, 2010). Balmer's study also showed that when controlling for different factors such as age and advice topic, telephone advice takes on average 14 minutes longer than face-to-face advice. Remote channels of advice provision will only take less time and lead to equal or better outcomes for certain people in certain circumstances. Restricting advice to telephone-based services for *all* cases could potentially act as a deterrent to people for whom this channel may not be suitable. As a result, further problems may accumulate or intensify, thus making them more costly to deal with in the long run.

The shift to digitised benefit services risks excluding certain people who lack the necessary IT access or skills to manage their claims online. Ofcom figures indicate that approximately 20% of the UK population does not have internet access at all, whilst 30% lack good-quality regular access at work, home or via a mobile device (Ofcom, 2012).

Groups commonly thought to be disproportionally represented within these figures include disabled people, those 65 years and older, people living in rural areas and people living on a low income. In addition, people who are thought to be digitally excluded – and therefore most at risk of being disadvantaged by the shift to digital channels – are often among those who are most likely to be applying for welfare services.

The government has recognised that some people may require assistance to access digital benefit services. However, there is a lack of clarity on who will be eligible to use these alternative services and what support will be available for people unable to use online services at all.

Recent research indicates that claimants are increasingly relying on Citizens Advice Bureaux to assist them in applying and managing their Universal Credit or Job Seeker's Allowance claim (Yates, 2015). This suggests that rather than leading to any genuine savings, the digitisation of welfare benefits could simply be transferring costs onto the advice sector.

Whist access to technology remains a crucial issue, a complex array of interconnected factors will play a role in determining if and how a person is able to use technology for advice or benefit purposes. Existing ICT inequalities must not simply be seen as 'gap' that can be closed simply by extending access. Instead focus must be awarded to how different groups of people actually engage with technology and the specific barriers they face. From this perspective we can begin to ask 'micro-level' questions such as about what equipment and support people have access to; how people's individual needs, circumstances and motivations affect their use of technology for advice or benefit purposes; and how different access points (such as libraries) either hinder or facilitate people's use of technology for these purposes. Drawing on interviews which were carried in 2014, in the following section I explore some of the specific implications of the digitisation of advice and benefit services for homeless people and the people that support them.

Accessing advice and information: a role for technology?

The interviews sought to explore homeless people's engagement with, and opinions of, technology for advice and information purposes. Several participants felt that the internet has a role to play in providing information:

'If I didn't have the internet, I wouldn't have known where to start, so I think, yeah, it is quite important that you have some sort of access, just so you can like find information out for yourself, because otherwise you're kind of left like clueless and then that makes you feel, like, oh God, I don't know where to go.' (Homeless male, aged 18–24)

Many homeless people felt there to be a lack of targeted and easily accessible information, particularly when first becoming homeless. Some participants who experienced difficulty in accessing appropriate support, reasoned that the internet could be used to better advertise and increase awareness of the location and nature of support services. In addition, some of the younger participants (aged 18–24) used Google Maps on their smartphones in order to locate organisations, which suggests that technology has a role to play in the early stages of people's advice journeys. However, once the participants located a support service, they expressed a clear preference for face-to-face advice:

'I liked coming in and talking to them, asking questions direct there, you know … they gave me confidence, you know, that someone's there looking after you at least, you're not alone, so they gave me confidence in that aspect. For someone to have knowledge of it, telling you made you feel a bit better. That's vital – safer, because out there you're alone and it's a cold world.' (Homeless male, aged 18–24)

The staff who were interviewed reiterated that face-to-face advice is particularly important when people are facing a crisis situation. In recent research carried out on behalf of Shelter, people experiencing housing issues also expressed a clear preference for face-to-face advice, as it was seen to meet their emotional as well as practical needs (TNS BRMB, 2015). For people experiencing a crisis situation such as homelessness, the complexity of the homelessness support system can be overwhelming, which in turn can make it difficult for people to express their needs:

'You need to be able to talk to a person, until they can come up with a robot that can talk to a person … they [people] can find out the nuances. Many of the people we see have an inability to communicate effectively what they want.' (Staff member, support service)

When attempting to access support, the homeless participants reported struggling to comprehend the various rules and procedures they encountered. This complexity and the sheer quantity of available information can limit the usefulness of telephone and online services in some instances:

'The eligibility requirements are quite complicated for all the services so while we want people on the one hand to have access to be able to make decisions themselves, actually what it often means is not empowering because there's so many different places you can go for so many different things. But actually what you need is for someone to say no that's the right one and to help them to make that decision.' (Staff member, support service)

Information is often a one-off communication of knowledge (for example on the location of support services), whereas advice is a more time-consuming process which generally includes suggestions being offered by the adviser on the best course of action. The different practices and preferences participants expressed in relation to advice and information suggests that there may be a need for a clearer differentiation between these two forms of support.

Interviews with staff from one local drop-in centre indicated that the reduction in face-to-face advice services is having an impact beyond the advice sector:

> 'We're dealing with different issues to what we were dealing with three or four years ago. People are coming to us for advice because there's nobody else out there that can offer advice. They don't like the formality of having to make an appointment to go to Citizen's Advice Bureau.' (Staff member, support service)

The chaotic lifestyles of some homeless people, along with a reduction in face-to-face services, causes staff and volunteers at some drop-in centres to have to provide fairly complex unofficial legal advice. This includes (but is not limited to) helping people fill out benefit application forms, making numerous phone calls to the LA or DWP to appeal homelessness and/or benefit decisions, making referrals to other agencies, and advising people about their rights and entitlements. This advice can take place on a very informal basis. At one day centre, staff can frequently be observed sitting on the floor of a busy common room whilst providing one-on-one assistance to guests in filling out a benefit application form.

Homeless people's experiences of a digitalised benefit service

At the time of the interviews, Universal Credit had not yet been rolled out into the local area. Many of the homeless people, however, spoke of their experiences or claiming JSA and using the Universal Jobmatch website.

Access barriers significantly affect homeless people's ability to successfully manage their JSA claims. Lacking internet access at home, some participants reported having to navigate their claims via their smartphones. Managing a benefit claim on a smartphone is a time-consuming and frustrating process, with screens often too small to navigate such a complex website. In addition, smartphones can be very slow at downloading and displaying a large amount of information.

Homeless people also face a number of barriers to using mobile phones, such as a shortage of places to charge the battery, whilst cost barriers can also restrict homeless people to expensive pay-as-you-go arrangements, which in turn limits regular use the internet.

Participants who managed their JSA claim on a desktop computer at a public access point or at a support organisation reported additional barriers such as restricted access, outdated equipment, slow or intermittent internet speeds and limited opening hours.

Some interviewees had limited or no prior experience of using computers or the internet when their claim was transferred online. The scale and speed with which the shift to online benefit claims and job searches has occurred carries significant implications for people who lack the necessary IT skills:

> At the job centre there's only one computer and that's just for job search not to train you up on computers ... it's like you're supposed to know everything like you were born with technology in your head.' (Homeless participant, age 55-64)

In addition, the interviews with support staff suggest that people with complex support needs or mental health problems require significant help in adapting to the channel shift:

> Arguably they are being forced to use computers that are completely alien to them and inevitably you will get a few who will totally refuse. There are always certain clients who flat out refuse to use computers and then that's it. Particularly if someone has mental health issues.' (Staff interview, support service)

Staff report that some people with limited IT experience and/or mental health problems can come to view computers and the internet with suspicion. In these instances the shift to online job searches can act as a disincentive to claiming JSA. People facing language or literacy issues were also said to require particularly high levels of support in managing their claims. The staff reported that resource constraints experienced by homelessness support services can, however, significantly limit the extent to which they are able to provide this level of support.

A number of homeless people who were interviewed reported that these barriers made it impossible for them to meet the conditions of their claim, which in turn resulted in them being sanctioned. These findings are supported by ongoing research at the University of Sheffield, which suggests that that homeless people are being disproportionally sanctioned, with ICT-related issues cited as key barriers (Beatty et al, 2015). This in turn can result in a wide array of negative consequences, such as poverty, survival crime, debt, mental health problems and homelessness.

Conclusion

Within the government's digitisation of advice and welfare benefits, the different factors which affect people's ability to use technology have not been adequately taken into account. By failing to recognise the various barriers, forms of use and circumstances of different group of people, all advice seekers and technology users are presented as one homogenised group. However, people use technology in multifaceted and variable ways, whilst encountering barriers which are specific to their own circumstances. The idea that all citizens can be served by one universal system can therefore be argued to be somewhat unrealistic. In order to avoid disadvantaging some of society's most vulnerable individuals, a 'one-size-fits-all' approach to digitisation must be abandoned in favour of an approach which recognises the diverse situations and experiences of different groups of people.

Notes

[1]   A client is exempt if in detention, under 18 years old or has recently been referred to face-to-face advice by the Gateway.

PART TWO
INTRODUCTION

Morag McDermont

The chapters in this part explore the experience of giving and receiving advice in a specific field, namely that of employment disputes. Here we draw on the stories of the 158 CAB clients who took part in one of the research projects, people who had approached their local Citizens Advice after experiencing a problem at work. When we began this research we were particularly interested in how the Employment Tribunal system did, or did not, function as a mechanism for accessing justice. We knew from a pilot research project that many found it an intimidating, highly legalised institution that was very difficult to engage in without specialist legal help. While our research confirmed this, it also confirmed the importance to many workers of the tribunal as a space independent from the workplace – a space where they could get their dispute heard.

Unfortunately, part-way through our research the landscape changed dramatically for workers with employment problems with the introduction of fees for taking a case to an Employment Tribunal. As Laura's story demonstrates (the case study that opens Part Two), the impact of having to pay a fee – which could be up to £1200 to get to a hearing for a more complex case – was to make access to the tribunal impossible for many. Laura's story has become the 'new normal', as Michael Ford says in his 'Reflection' which follows.

Michael provides a barrister's perspective on the impact of fees, drawing on his many years' experience of representing workers in complex legal cases at Employment Tribunals, along with a detailed analysis of the government's own statistics which show the dramatic decline in applications following the introduction of fees.

Chapter Four provides a summary of the legal provisions that create numerous challenges, and barriers, for those seeking to access the ET system, starting from the historical perspective of Industrial Tribunals and the principles they attempted to establish of easily accessible and affordable routes to justice. Chapter Five returns to the research data to explore two key questions through the eyes of advisers and their clients: how do people think about the law in relation to problems at work, or disputes with their employers, and how do advisers transform or augment these notions into action or inaction in relation to employment disputes? Chapter Six concludes this part with a sociologist's perspective, using the workers' stories to explore the precarity, insecurity and inequality experienced by many workers, and the importance in this respect of the CAB advisers who attempt to negotiate settlements with employers.

'LAURA': THE EFFECT OF FEES UPON THE EMPLOYMENT TRIBUNAL PROCESS

Case study compiled by Eleanor Kirk

Laura worked for a retail company for six years before she was suspended over an alleged incident which she denied, providing evidence to support her innocence. However, when she learned that there was a fee to be paid for submitting a claim, and for holding a hearing, this was a 'gamble' she felt unable to take.

The story

Laura worked in a large supermarket chain for more than six years. A store security guard filmed Laura on CCTV going to her car during her break. He claimed she was taking illegal drugs. Laura states that she was taking a hay fever remedy. After returning to work from being in her car, Laura was approached by a manager and informed that she was suspended. She asked the reason for this and was told it was due to the incident that happened earlier in the evening. At the time, Laura did not know what incident was being referred to. The next day she received a letter from her employer informing her that she had been suspended because she was working under the influence of illegal drugs.

Laura vehemently denied she had been taking illegal drugs. She contacted her employer and offered to have a drug test taken immediately, as it was still within the appropriate time period that would make this valid. The employer declined her offer. Laura then had her own test taken, which showed that she had not been under the influence of illegal drugs. Laura had a disciplinary meeting. Laura was not a member of a union. In line with its own policy, the employer provided two staff representatives to attend the meeting with Laura. These representatives were not union representatives, and Laura felt that they had insufficient training on store procedure or employment law. One of the representatives indicated to Laura that the matter was above her head and that she did not have a clue how to help fight it for her. Laura offered her drug test results to prove her innocence. The manager informed her that they did not need any further proof as their evidence on the matter showed "beyond reasonable doubt" that she was taking illegal drugs. Laura was fired from her job. She appealed this decision, but the employer upheld it, saying that her dismissal was justified.

In her first meeting at the CAB, Laura felt confident that she had a strong case. She had studied the employer's disciplinary and dismissal procedures and had identified numerous breaches of procedure by her manager. She had arranged for a trade union rep to come with her to the appeal meeting, who was very encouraging, telling her:

'I'd have thought that'd help and when we come out of the meeting he says, "Laura, that couldn't have gone any better, that meeting", because I pointed out all the wrongs that they'd done. I'd done everything I could to prove that they were wrong and he says "That couldn't have gone any better". He says, "So I hope, like, you do well in it", and they wrote to me and said, "No, sorry, we're sticking with the thingy, dismissal".'

As matters progressed Laura became significantly more downcast and pessimistic about her prospect of successfully challenging her dismissal. She had learnt that she would need to pay ET fees of £250 to lodge a claim and then a further £950 to have her claim heard. She was not eligible for remission because she was in receipt of contribution-based Employment and Support Allowance. Laura felt that there was nothing more she could do to deal with the situation because she could not afford to pay the fees:

> At the end of the day ... I could've won and I might not have done. I haven't got £1100 to pay on something I might not win. ... I'm on my own with two children without a job at the moment ... If I knew I could claim my money back ... even if I lost, at least I've got that money back, I would've been okay, you know, I would've been a bit gutted but I would've been all right. But I can't afford to pay over £1000 for something which is a gamble. I might as well just go to the bookies.

Laura had contacted various lawyers to see if she might get not only representation but someone who might front the tribunal fees. A solicitor who was already a personal contact told her:

> "'I'm willing to give you advice", [Laura], she says, "but all I can do is basically" ... she charged £190 an hour, that solicitor I saw, and she said, "Even if you won, you'd probably owe it all to me by the time we got to court anyway". So there's no point going down that route either.

Laura felt aggrieved. She had wanted to fight her case, but felt that she was denied the opportunity to do so. Laura had been advised by Acas, the solicitors and union representatives with whom she had consulted that she had a strong legal case for unfair dismissal. She had made many efforts to prove her innocence and fight for her cause, but felt that the power was firmly on the side of her employer and that she could not do anything about this. She had undertaken research and sought advice about her employer's human resources policies and relevant employment law, she had put a number of written questions to her employer in her appeal hearing but the employer's written response simply ignored many of these. She had also looked up regulation relating to workplace use of CCTV and had lodged a complaint with the Surveillance Camera Commissioner. However, the reality of her situation was that she was struggling financially and still without a job. She had applied for a number of positions, but was finding it virtually impossible to obtain work because she now no longer had a clean employment record. Indeed, Laura did not even know the detail of what her previous employment record stated.

A family member suggested that she obtain copies of her file from her former employer, "to see what exactly they're gonna put on me … you know, if a new job rang for me, for a reference, I want to see what's on my personnel files, to be honest, to see what they're putting on there". Laura was preparing to do so at last contact with the research project.

Ultimately, it seemed that there was little she could do now, and she felt deprived of access to justice:

> I'm gutted because I wanted to fight 'em … They were wrong in what they did. They didn't give you any chance to prove your own innocence … it's all just a big, massive cover up and there's not a single thing I can do about it … I can't clear my name and I'm struggling getting a job at the moment.

A REFLECTION ON CASE STUDY TWO: LAURA AND THE EFFECT OF FEES

Michael Ford QC[*]

Laura's decision not to take her case to tribunal would be a fairly familiar story even before the introduction of tribunal fees. A large-scale survey conducted in the late 1990s found that 16% of workers with legal problems related to employment did nothing about them, higher than the corresponding percentages for justiciable problems relating to family, consumer or housing matters; the reasons for no action included that the workers thought nothing could be done about it, because they were scared, or owing to the cost, time and trouble involved (Genn, 1999: 43-4). These difficulties remain and are exacerbated by other factors: workers who are not union members have limited practical access to legal advice and legal costs are prohibitive; the legal cards are often stacked against claimants; tribunals have a very limited role in assisting claimants who represent themselves, and those without representation are significantly disadvantaged; tribunal awards have always small and difficult to enforce. If those were not sufficient obstacles already, fees add another barrier.

[*] Michael Ford QC is Professor of Law, University of Bristol and a fee-paid Employment Judge. He is Counsel for the Equality and Human Rights Commission in the judicial review case challenging the legality of Employment Tribunal fees.

Unfair dismissal: problems before fees

In theory dismissals for conduct outside working hours, such as Laura's, give rise to interesting questions about how the law on unfair dismissal applies to conduct outside working time, including in light of Article 8 of the European Convention on Human Rights. The reality for a worker in her position is rather more mundane. An employment tribunal would not investigate whether she actually committed the act of misconduct for the purpose of unfair dismissal, and would simply direct itself to consider whether the decision to dismiss was one which a reasonable employer might take based on the evidence before it.[1] If there was breach of the employer's internal procedure of the sort Laura identified before her appeal, the tribunal would reduce her compensation if she still might have been fairly dismissed in any case – the so-called *Polkey*[2] deduction, which is a very common means by which unfairly dismissed employees end up with little compensation.

As a result, compensation for those who succeed in unfair dismissal claims, which is the only remedy available in practice,[3] has always been low. In each of the financial years from 2007 to 2013, for example, the median award for unfair dismissal was less than £5000.[4] Not content with this empirical reality and the existing monetary ceiling on the compensatory award,[5] in 2012 the Coalition government relied upon 'unrealistic perceptions [*sic*] among both employees and employers about the level of tribunal awards' as the basis for subjecting the compensatory award to a further cap of a maximum of one year's salary.[6] It ignored evidence from its own extensive survey of employment tribunal applicants that the median amount claimants hoped for – their perception – was only £5000 (BIS, 2013b: 26, referring to BIS, 2010), and rather than trying to correct false perceptions among employers opted instead to penalise employees. The effect of this new cap is felt above all by low earners (especially part-time workers) whose dismissal would make it hard for them to find another job quickly, such as Laura.

Unusually for a non-union member, Laura was fortunate enough to receive some legal advice. But her solicitor was no doubt right to tell her that the costs of legal representation would almost certainly absorb all or most of any unfair dismissal compensation. The hearing itself would take a day at least; add to that preparation time, including the now routine production of written witness statements, and her solicitor's costs would be very significant. Although costs orders are more common than they once were[7] – a reflection of the increasing isomorphism of ETs and ordinary courts – they remain the exception not the rule, restricted to unreasonable conduct or the pursuit of allegations with no reasonable prospects of success.[8] However strong Laura's case on, for example, procedural unfairness, her employer would no doubt contend that it was reasonable to contest the claim for the purpose of disputes about matters such as *Polkey* deductions and the level of compensation, so that no costs order would be made. In 2014/15, for instance, only 335 costs awards of over £1000 were made in favour of claimants, a period in which ETs disposed of 18,839 single claims.[9] The restricted scope for costs protects claimants, of course; but it has the effect of making it economically difficult for lawyers to represent them, even where the case appears very strong, unless the claimant is a high earner.

Workers who succeed in the employment tribunal and receive an award of compensation then face the problem of receiving the money. Perhaps as a former employee of a large supermarket chain Laura would not face this further obstacle. But many successful tribunal claimants are not so fortunate. In the course of the first judicial review proceedings challenging fees,[10] the Lord Chancellor referred to BIS research into the payment of tribunal awards, conducted before fees were introduced (BIS, 2013c). Without the use of enforcement, 41% of claimants were paid in full and 53% in part; after using enforcement 66% were paid at least something (at page 7). The authors noted that this was 'a particular concern' in light of the forthcoming introduction of fees (at page 7) because a successful claimant would need to chase the employer for the fees, making claimants the effective guarantors of the system. But their warnings went unheeded, with the Ministry of Justice glibly responding to this issue in the consultation by stating that 'we expect all parties to abide by the decision of the tribunal and pay the awards and fees as ordered' (MoJ, 2012: 26, para 94). Instead of improving enforcement for claimants, the government has since focused on introducing financial penalties payable to the Secretary of State by recalcitrant employers,[11] with no significant effect to date.[12]

The dramatic effect of fees

This dismal picture is now overshadowed by fees, introduced with effect from 30 July 2013 by the Employment Tribunals and Employment Appeals Tribunal Fees Order 2013.[13] According to the government's publication which announced (without prior consultation) the future imposition of fees along with other reforms aimed at reducing the regulatory burden of employment law, a 'price mechanism could help ... to disincentivise unreasonable behaviour, like pursuing weak or vexatious claims' (BIS, 2011: 50).[14] But the rational economic agent relied on by the government should know that even if she won her claim and received judgment for a most likely small amount of compensation coupled with an order that the employer repays her fees,[15] she may well not recover either. Fees are an extremely blunt weapon with which to attack vexatious or speculative litigants because the collateral damage extends to those with limited resources, those bringing claims for small sums or those, such as many discrimination claimants, who cannot readily assess the strength of their claim in advance because of a lack of evidence.[16] The available data indicates the wide impact of the collateral damage. In giving the lead judgment in the Court of Appeal in *R (Unison) v Lord Chancellor (Nos. 1 and 2)* [2016] ICR 1, Underhill LJ referred to statistics showing a 79% decline in all claims.[17] The latest tribunal statistics for the period July to September 2015 confirm this, showing a 72% drop in mean single claims per quarter since fee charging commenced.[18] Both of these figures are based solely on claims issued, and ignore the further significant deterrent effect of the more substantial hearing fees.[19] No evidence has been produced by the government to show the deterrent effect is on weak claims because none exists.

Laura's story is typical of this larger picture. Her unfair dismissal claim requires the higher Type B fee of £230 on issue of the claim and £950 before the hearing. Just like Laura, many potential claimants have just lost their jobs and are already in financial difficulties, and few will obtain remission. A potential claimant is ineligible for remission if her and her partner's 'disposable capital' is £3000 or more, including non-monetary assets which can be sold (less 10% of their market value) with the exception of items such as the dwelling house and its effects, clothing and an essential motor vehicle, but not notice and redundancy payments.[20] While the Lord Chancellor has power to waive fees in exceptional circumstances, it is unclear whether this power has in fact been exercised.[21] The result is that the number of remissions is far lower than the last government's analysis before fees, based on the old remission system, which predicted about 23% of the then claimant population would obtain remission.[22] For the year 2014/15 the latest statistics show that 19,398 issue fees were requested for single claims, of which 4074 claimants, or 21%, were granted remission. But this is 21% of the post-claims population; given the decline in single claims of about 72%, it amounts to no more than about 6% of the claims issued pre-fees.

Laura's claim is typical in a further respect: the reason why she withdrew her claim had nothing to do with the actual or perceived strength of her case but because of financial difficulties and a feeling of helplessness. This too is borne out by the statistical information. If fees deterred weak claims in accordance with the government's rationale for a price mechanism, one would predict an increase in the success rate of the claims post-fees. Yet the statistics on ET disposals for 2014/15, which include mostly cases heard in respect of which claimants paid fees,[23] show no discernible change in the success rate of cases which went to a hearing, regardless of whether the focus is on all claims or on individual types of claim.[24]

It is a plausible hypothesis that fees have not especially deterred vexatious claimants - such claimants may be less susceptible to economic steering or other disincentives - but have instead deterred for other, independent reasons, just as in Laura's case. Anecdotal evidence suggests that small wages claims brought by single individuals have all but disappeared.[25] Research based on claimants who were subject both to fees and to the now compulsory Acas early conciliation scheme found that, where conciliation did not achieve a settlement, by far the most common reason for not submitting a tribunal claim was the fee (26%), followed by the issue having been resolved (20%) (Downer et al, 2015: 97–8). Asked why the fee was off-putting, 68% of claimants said they could not afford it, 19% said it was more than they were prepared to pay and 9% said it equalled the money owed. Non-members of trade unions were especially liable to be deterred (at 97–8). This research confirms the preliminary findings of the Survey of Employment Tribunal Applications in 2013, based on asking a large sample of tribunal claimants about a hypothetical fee of £250, that it would affect the decision of about half to go to tribunal, with the effect greatest on temporary staff, those with lower income and those with low-value claims – but not those who ultimately lost at hearing (BIS 2013a: 38–41).

Laws without enforcement

Long before fees were introduced, the difficulties faced by claimants led to strong criticisms of individual litigation and calls for the greater use of ADR (Alternative Dispute Resolution) or other methods to ensure practical delivery of labour standards, often under the fashionable label of 'reflexive' regulation (see for example Hepple, 2012). The premise was, naturally, that the system should deliver on the duties of equality, fairness and the like to which it was implicitly committed (Dickens, 2012). The main reason for introducing fees side-steps the premise: the primary aim is budgetary – as it was put in the consultation documents, to save 23% of the Ministry of Justice's budget, to reduce the financial burdens on the taxpayer and to bring tribunals into line with the government policy of charging for publicly provided services (see BIS, 2011; MoJ, 2012). Though said to involve a 'balance' between reducing the burden on the taxpayer and 'access to justice for all' (BIS, 2011: 3), the access envisaged is theoretical not practical, and economic imperatives determine where the balance is struck.

The effect of fees will give a real-life test to the many criticisms of the system's reliance on individual rights and individual claims. For what happens when individual claims radically reduce, to the point where the risk of claims is small? What will be the wider effects then on labour standards? Based on a model of how pricing mechanisms affect individual behaviour, the Government's analysis paid scant attention to this wider, public function of tribunal claims. At present, with the principal exceptions of health and safety and the national minimum wage, there is virtually no agency enforcement of labour standards. In the absence of individual claims, the 'reflexive' approach which remains is encouragement and exhortation. As the Ministry of Justice put it in rejecting any wider societal impacts resulting from fewer claims, 'the Government supports a wide range of guidance, advice provision and help-lines which help businesses to observe their legal responsibilities' (MoJ, 2012: 18, para 54). So no doubt does everyone; we may only miss individual claims when they are dead.

Though 'troubled' by the decline of claims post-fees, ultimately the Court of Appeal in *Unison* was not clear if this was the result of potential claimants' inability or unwillingness to pay.[26] The boundary between these two categories is elusive if not to say nonexistent, and it is unclear where or how the law should draw the line. The court's binary logic does not capture the other problems faced by claimants in the ET which fees exacerbate, such as evidential difficulties in discrimination claims or the problem of recovering compensation and fees. On 26 February 2016 Unison was given permission to appeal to the Supreme Court, and we await the government's review into fees, promised from the first judicial review and still outstanding,[27] so the story is not over. This is all too late for Laura, and many thousands of other claimants. Her story is the new normal, of what I have termed regulatory *laissez-faire*: legal rights to which the government is opposed, which it cannot repeal owing to EU law or which it considers politically imprudent to remove from the statute book for the moment,[28] but which it knows can be undermined by procedural reforms falling under the convenient justification of 'austerity'. I suspect research into areas of precarious work, such as agency work, will confirm the utter irrelevance of regulation in practice, just as the existing data on the effect of fees would predict.[29]

Notes

[1] This is so even if a claim potentially gives rise to issues based on Article 8: see especially *Turner v East Midlands Trains* [2013] ICR 525. In practical terms, it is hard to find a single case where Article 8 has made a difference to an unfair dismissal claim: see e.g. *O'Flynn v Airlinks* EAT/0269/01.

[2] *Polkey v AE Dayton Services* [1988] AC 344.

[3] In 2014/15, of 2655 claims for unfair dismissal which succeeded, a total of five orders of reinstatement or reengagement were made: see Table E.2 to MoJ, *Tribunal and Gender Recognition Certificate Statistics Quarterly, April to June 2015* (10 September 2015).

[4] See MoJ, *Tribunal and Gender Recognition Certificate Statistics Quarterly, April to June 2015* (10 September 2015), Table E.4.

[5] Currently just over £78,000 – a sum of little relevance to most successful claimants.

[6] See BIS (2012: 25) and, now, section 124(ZA) of the Employment Rights Act 1996, introduced by the Unfair Dismissal (Variation of the Limits of the Compensatory Award) Order 2013/1949.

[7] See Table E.12 in *Tribunal and Gender Recognition Certificate Statistics Quarterly, April to June 2015*, above.

[8] See rule 76 of the Employment Tribunal (Constitution and Rules of Procedure) Regulations 2013 and for example *Yerraklava v Barnsley MBC* [2012] ICR 420.

[9] See *Tribunal and Gender Recognition Certificate Statistics Quarterly, April to June 2015*, above, Tables 2.2 and E.12.

[10] *R (Unison) v Lord Chancellor* [2014] ICR 498.

[11] See section 16 of the Enterprise and Regulatory Reform Act 2013, which came into force on 6 April 2014, introducing a new section 12A into ERA 1996 which provides for penalties for 'aggravated' breach of employment rights, and section 150 of the Small Business, Enterprise and Employment Act 2015, due to come into force in April 2016, providing for penalties where an employer does not pay a tribunal award or an agreed settlement.

[12] One year after the introduction of section 12A ERA 1996, a grand total of three orders had been made, *one* of which had been paid: see the Written Answer by Nick Boles in Parliament on 8 June 2015 (Question No. 133).

[13] SI 2013 No. 1892.

[14] See too the similar objectives in the subsequent consultation on the mechanics of charging fees, (MoJ, 2011: 14–15).

[15] See rules 74–76 of the Tribunal Rules of Procedure.

[16] The difficulties of proof in discrimination claims have long been recognised, flowing from the fact that evidence of overt discrimination is rarely available: see for example *Chattopadhyay v Headmaster of Holloway School* [1982] ICR 132. It is precisely for such reasons that the burden of proof is reversed in both the EU Directives in this field and in section 139 of the Equality Act 2010.

[17] See paragraph 62.

[18] Ministry of Justice, *Tribunal and Gender Recognition Certificate Statistics Quarterly, October to December 2015* (10 March 2016), Table 1.2. The 72% drop is based on comparing the figures for (i) the quarters from 2009/10 until the first quarter of

2013/14 (before fees) with (ii) the corresponding figures post-fees, from the third quarter of 2013/14 until the third quarter of 2015/16. Multiple claims have been excluded because they are more liable to volatility based on large claims for many claimants (such as holiday pay or equal pay claims); quarter 2 for 2013/14, from July to September 2013, has been excluded from the calculation because it includes claims both pre- and post-fees.

[19] See the experimental statistics in Table D.2, Ministry of Justice, *Tribunal and Gender Recognition Certificate Statistics Quarterly, October to December 2015* (10 March 2016). Though a little opaque, they illustrate that a further significant proportion of claimants do not pay the hearing fee, do not obtain remission or do not settle their case. The data do not show the number of claims dismissed under rule 40 because of a failure to pay the hearing fee.

[20] See Schedule 3 to the Fees Order, especially at paragraphs 3, 6 and 10.

[21] See Schedule 3, paragraph 16 to the Fees Order.

[22] See *Impact Assessment: Introducing a Fee Charging Regime in the Employment Tribunals and Employment Appeal Tribunal* (30 May 2012), paragraph 4.17, page 26. The Impact Assessment for the new scheme acknowledged it would reduce eligibility but did not assess the number of ET claimants who would be eligible: see *Impact Assessment: Court and Tribunal Fee Remission Reform* (9 September 2013).

[23] The mean time for disposal of a single claim is currently 29 weeks – see *Tribunal and Gender Recognition Statistics Quarterly, October to December 2015*, page 20 – but it was 38 weeks between April and June 2014: see *Tribunal Statistics Quarterly, April to June 2014* (11 September 2014), page 18. Claims issued after 30 July 2013 would be disposed of, on average, from around April 2014.

[24] See Table 2.3 of the October to December 2015 statistics, *Tribunal and Gender Recognition Statistics Quarterly, October to December 2015*, page 20.

[25] This is not captured by the official statistics because they do not break down jurisdictional claims into single and multiple claims – and many claims for wages will have been brought as part of the recent large multiples for holiday pay claims, following the ruling of the Court of Justice in *Williams v British Airways* [2012] ICR 847: see on this Table 1.2 to the *Tribunal and Gender Recognition Statistics Quarterly, October to December 2015*

[26] Per Underhill LJ at paragraph 68.

[27] See the written evidence of the Ministry of Justice to the Justice Committee at http://data.parliament.uk/writtenevidence/committeeevidence.svc/evidencedocument/justice-committee/courts-and-tribunals-fees-and-charges/written/21907.html.

[28] Compare the Beecroft (2011), *Report on Employment Law* commissioned by the Coalition government which, as well as advocating the introduction of 'no fault' dismissal, also made clear its general opposition to labour market regulation in general, going so far as to suggest the government should break the law by not implementing the Agency Workers Directive.

[29] See BIS (2013a) and the Agency Workers Regulations 2010.

4

THE COSTS OF JUSTICE: BARRIERS AND CHALLENGES TO ACCESSING THE EMPLOYMENT TRIBUNAL SYSTEM

Nicole Busby[*]

Introduction

In its previous guise as the Industrial Tribunal, the Employment Tribunal was intended to provide an 'easily accessible, speedy, informal and inexpensive' route to workplace dispute resolution (Royal Commission on Trade Unions and Employers' Associations, 1968). Whether that ideal was ever achievable is open to debate but it certainly cannot be claimed for the institution that we know today. Alongside the name change, the current specialist tribunal has undergone a series of fundamental reforms – some in recent years – which have taken it ever

[*] Nicole Busby is Professor of Labour Law at the University of Strathclyde. In her research she explores labour market regulation and its socioeconomic context. Her recent work focuses on the relationship between paid work and unpaid care, the constitutionalisation of labour rights and claimants' experiences of the UK's Employment Tribunal system.

further away from this vision. As well as being a legalistic, adversarial and often very formal arena, the service it provides to individuals who find themselves embroiled in workplace disputes is no longer free. The imposition of fees for claimants in July 2013 has been widely criticised as representing an insurmountable barrier to access to justice for many workers, making the ET unaffordable and thus preventing the effective use of a range of employment rights such as protection against unfair dismissal and discrimination and the basic right to claim unpaid wages for work already performed. However, even before the introduction of fees, many claimants found the experience of pursuing an ET claim extremely difficult, resulting in high personal and financial costs. Feelings of bewilderment and alienation are often reported by those embroiled in a highly legalistic process, particularly if self-representing. Coupled with the psychological and financial effects of an ongoing dispute with an (often former) employer, such barriers increasingly mean that many with potentially viable claims decide to walk away rather than to pursue a resolution.

I will explore in this chapter the challenges encountered by those seeking to access the ET system, with a particular focus on those claimants who do not have trade union support and who cannot easily afford to pay for legal advice and representation. The aim of the chapter is to identify the costs of justice in this context and to suggest how such costs might best be met. Some of the current difficulties arise due to certain systemic features which, despite contributing to the negative experiences of claimants, are an inherent consequence of attempting to provide legal redress in this area. However, what is largely missing from the current provision is consideration for the needs of claimants – particularly those who lack representation – and it is this aspect which will provide the focus as I explore how an improved service might be achieved. It is argued that it is only by acknowledging the many foibles of the current system and attempting to counter them through enhanced support mechanisms that access to justice will be achievable for all.

The Employment Tribunal: principles and purpose

As well as delivering a system that would be 'easily accessible, speedy, informal and inexpensive', the Donovan Report's (Royal Commission on Trade Unions and Employers' Associations, 1968) recommendations also laid the foundations for today's unfair dismissal legislation which was implemented in Britain by the Industrial Relations Act 1971 by a Conservative government led by Edward Heath. The legal right to be protected against unfair dismissal endures but it has been reshaped through the years by political and judicial responses to the changing socioeconomic context within which the labour market operates. This illustrates a critical point about the ET which, more so than any other adjudicative body, makes decisions daily on 'big picture' issues of social and economic policy that, as well as inculcating the relevant legislative and common law principles, must reflect the fast-changing environment within which the exchange of labour and wages takes place. Furthermore, and perhaps most importantly, the disputes that it considers involve an activity that is of central importance to individual workers which is inextricably linked to financial and psychological wellbeing and which provides a crucial component of individual identity. Given that the ET performs such an important role with obvious implications for public health, workplace harmony and, consequently, economic prosperity, one might imagine that its successful operation would be a matter of the utmost priority for policy makers and it has certainly been the focus of much deliberation in recent years. However, despite a succession of government-commissioned reviews, there still seems to be a lack of consensus among politicians regarding the future of the ET.

Our research considered the perceptions and experiences of individuals with potential claims (see NSLC, 2016). We made contact with our research participants through their local Citizens Advice Bureaux where, without any other form of available support, they had gone for advice concerning an employment-related dispute. We followed these individuals over four years as they attempted to reach resolution in various ways. Most of our participants experienced the tribunal system at some level: some only got as far as submitting the ET1 form to lodge their claim, others engaged with conciliation using the service provided by Acas or reached negotiated settlements through other means, and a small number ended up at a full hearing.

We collected over 150 stories which together paint an interesting and complex picture. As our findings illustrate, claimants experience the system in different ways depending on the range of resources – legal, social and financial – at their disposal. Unsurprisingly, those without access to legal advice and representation often have the most difficult journeys and do not always stay the course. With stretched and dwindling budgets, CABx are not always able to offer much more than case preparation so that, increasingly, claimants are left to represent themselves at hearings. Although the advent of fees has exacerbated the difficulties claimants face, they are by no means the sole cause of those difficulties. In fact, many of the cases we tracked predated the introduction of ET fees in July 2013. So what factors constitute the main barriers and challenges to access to justice in the ET?

The law

The complexity of employment law is well recognised within and beyond the legal profession itself. As well as a detailed understanding of the complex web of domestic legislative and common law provisions and an up-to-date knowledge of their interpretation by tribunals and courts, a specialist practitioner is required to be familiar with the highly technical area of EU employment law which is part of the UK framework. The first job of any legal adviser would be to identify the law which is relevant to the employment dispute. It is unlikely that many people without such specialist knowledge would be able to fully understand terms such as 'constructive dismissal', 'breach of contract', 'equal pay' or 'discrimination', never mind relate the relevant law to their particular situation. In this sense, law remains 'out there', relevant only in a very vague way to the individual claimant. Where a solicitor or advice worker is able to provide support to run the case on the claimant's behalf, this might not matter so much. However, where individual claimants have to deal themselves with tribunal processes, ignorance of the law can have consequences, which may be only partly offset by judges' attempts to make hearings less formal.

Pre-hearing procedures

Although a basic awareness of the existence of certain employment rights might be high among the general population, most remain unaware of the standard path required to invoke such rights. This is not surprising – we tend to take the regular payment of our wages for granted and employment protection and anti-discrimination legislation is only relevant when we need to use it. Many of those who do need to engage in the process do so with little or no knowledge of how to go about it or of possible subsequent courses of action should their efforts fail to produce results. Despite the detailed guidance offered by the Courts and Tribunal Service itself, many participants remained unaware of its existence or talked of its inadequacy in helping them to navigate what is experienced as a complex path at a particularly stressful time. Contributory factors can be the timescales and involvement of various third parties.

Timescales

Despite the apparent simplicity of submitting an ET1 online to start a case, the timescales involved in pursuing a claim were experienced as problematic. Advisers understand the need for due process in legal matters and, in fact, some of the time limits imposed at various stages of the process are not particularly long, for example, the employer will have to respond to the ET1 within 28 days of receiving it. However, at a time of stress and with a high degree of personal investment – both emotional and financial – many participants feel that the process is defined by a sense of waiting. This can take several forms: waiting for the Acas conciliation process to reach its conclusion, waiting for the employer to act, waiting to hear back from an adviser, or for news from the Courts and Tribunal Service.

Third party involvement

From the claimant's viewpoint the case starts out as a dispute, however entrenched, with his or her employer. However, once embroiled in the claims process, the individual often has to liaise with a range of different organisations and personnel. For the unrepresented claimant this can be a cause of confusion and stress. Some of the participants in our research were unsure of their own role and what was expected of them during the process and had difficulty understanding the roles of their adviser, the Acas conciliator or the ET itself.

The role of Acas

Acas's participation can be a particular source of confusion for some claimants. Many start their claim following a call to the free Acas Helpline when they are given initial advice about their rights and how to go about invoking them. However, following the introduction of Early Conciliation (EC) in 2014, what is perceived as a shift in Acas's role during the process can be bewildering. Although Acas has always offered conciliation in employment cases, the new scheme makes it mandatory for potential claimants to contact Acas before initiating a claim. An attempt to conciliate an agreement is then made which can result in a binding settlement (a COT3 agreement) or in the issue of a certificate to the claimant, who can then lodge a claim with the ET by submitting an ET1. EC involves the assignment of a Conciliation Officer, who rightly takes a neutral and impartial stance and is unable to offer advice to the claimant, who might be embroiled in complex negotiations involving the terms of a settlement. Of course to the trained eye, EC and the Helpline service are separate Acas functions but this demarcation is not always understood by claimants. Furthermore, EC's description as 'The free, fast and less stressful alternative to an employment tribunal for resolving workplace disputes' on the notification page leads many to believe that it is an alternative to legal advice and representation. Although in some cases this may be true, a lack of knowledge about how to participate in negotiations and what to expect in terms of outcome can leave claimants feeling vulnerable and alone.

It is also worth considering the suitability of conciliation, particularly with regard to the more contentious types of cases. Conciliation is a neutral process which is not concerned with the quality of the outcome or settlement and the measure of success is merely that both parties agree on the outcome. It is not concerned with the justness of that agreement. There is, thus, an implicit but clear assumption that parties know their legal rights and understand the implications of the settlement.

These reservations aside, it should be noted that EC is certainly not perceived or experienced as a negative process by users. The admittedly small number of our research participants who used the scheme were happy with the service provided. Of particular note were the efforts made by Conciliation Officers to communicate the status of the negotiations at various stages.

Fees and remission

Fees for claimants were introduced on 29 July 2013. These are charged at two levels depending on the nature of the claim and are payable at two stages—on lodging the claim and before the hearing itself. The total costs for going to full hearing are: Type A claims (including unpaid wages) £390 and Type B claims (including unfair dismissal and discrimination claims) £1200. Remission - a partial or full fee waiver - is available in limited circumstances based on the worker's and/ or their household's financial details. Our research project has limited data on the effect of fees on individual decision making as most of the cases we followed predated their imposition. However the overall reduction in claims nationally, which has generally been calculated as around 70%, tells us that they present a barrier to pursuing claims and the reasons for this are obvious.

Workers who have recently lost their jobs are generally not in a position to pay to take a case to the ET. This is particularly so if their previous work was low waged, they are unemployed and/or it is likely that their future employment will also be low waged. Even those who consider or who have been advised that they have a strong case recognise that there is always the risk of losing on the day, which means that they face an often unacceptable risk of losing any fees they pay.

As well as such practical considerations, fees are likely to have an additional psychological effect on potential claimants. We discerned a sense of disaffectedness amongst some workers who felt that fees restricted their ability to pursue their claims, viewing themselves and their co-workers as having less and less power in comparison with employers. Despite having suffered a perceived wrong, some felt powerless to seek a remedy. A common observation is captured in the words of one individual:

> 'Well as far as I'm concerned, for me, there is no law or legal system … as far it is me getting justice, you know. You've got to pay for justice. What sort of justice is that?' (Tom)

For many, fees were viewed as part of broader trends towards a reduction in the rights of ordinary working people. For example, the increasing use of zero hours contracts, although legal, was identified as being highly problematic for workers:

> 'The ordinary working man … there's no rights. The laws are there but everybody's breaking them. Zero hour contracts … Nobody can get a mortgage on a zero hour contract. Nobody can get a car insurance on a zero hour contract' (Mother, accompanying Laura to her CAB meeting)

The hearing

Interestingly, although only a small minority of our research participants actually went all the way to a full hearing at the ET, once reached this stage tended to be less stressful than the path to it. This is not to deny that the prospect of appearing before a judge in what was assumed would be a 'court-like' environment was a cause of great concern:

almost all participants who faced the prospect were apprehensive about it. In advance of the hearing, few had a good sense of the process involved or what would be expected of them. Many were concerned about their ability to engage with unfamiliar language and concepts and worried that they would not be able to communicate what had happened to them in a meaningful and articulate manner.

Our findings indicate that ET judges generally attempt to ensure that participants do have their say and can be particularly skilful in encouraging and translating the use of everyday language into legal concepts in order for them to apply the law. However, despite such useful interventions, unrepresented claimants in particular can still experience the hearing as both bewildering and intimidating, with some unsure of the outcome even when present as judgment was given on the day.

The adversarial nature of the hearing

Claimants' perception of the ET as 'court-like' is not inaccurate. Despite its name, the ET has more in common with the civil court than with its fellow tribunals in the way in which the hearing is conducted. As a 'party to party' adversarial process the hearing can be a combative and contentious forum in which the employer – often through legal representatives – will fight to defend their position. Where this takes place before the judge, attempts will generally be made to remain polite and courteous. Even then, the experience of being cross-examined by a lawyer on the employer's behalf can be a very unpleasant experience. However, away from the judge's gaze, employers and their representatives can sometimes engage in unscrupulous game playing using intimidating tactics. For example, threats that an unsuccessful claimant will have to pay the employer's, costs can be made in waiting rooms or in the lead-up to the case, and purposefully stalling in the provision of paperwork so that the claimant has less time to prepare for the hearing is not uncommon.

Enforcement of awards

In successful claims which result in the ET making a financial award, it can come as a surprise that claimants do not automatically receive their remedy. Many have to take further steps – sometimes involving court action - to enforce, which can involve further cost. The outcomes for our participants in this respect echoed the findings from research carried out in 2013 by the Department for Business, Innovation & Skills (BIS) into the payment of ET awards (BIS, 2013c). The BIS study revealed that only half (49%) of claimants were paid their award in full and a further 16% were paid in part. The comparative percentages for our participants were 63% and 6% respectively. Overall, a similar percentage received all or some of their award (65% in the BIS study compared with 69% in ours). Sometimes a letter from the claimant's solicitor or adviser can be enough to procure payment but often further reserves of perseverance and determination as well as financial outlay might be required at the end of what has already been a difficult and stressful process.

Conclusions

As I have shown in this chapter, despite the existence of a range of well-established employment rights and the provision of a specialist tribunal, there are many reasons why workers may be reluctant or unable to pursue potentially viable claims against employers. Even those who do so are often left without any sense of having achieved justice, not least because of the difficulties in enforcing awards. For many it is easier to simply walk away. However, being prevented from pursuing justice can have ongoing negative effects for workers. In particular, a worker can be left with an inexplicable 'blemish' on their employment record, such as an unexplained departure from a job with no reference available. This can be especially problematic for those in low waged and low to unskilled work. The current economic climate, together with government policies encouraging those on benefits to take up work, mean that many employers have an available pool of workers to choose from. The negative psychological effect of having lost one's job and facing unemployment can make it difficult for people to actively seek work. Not being able to find work may result in reliance on benefits, which in turn can have negative consequences for an individual's outlook and self-esteem.

At the time of writing the government is engaged in a review of ET fees and is also considering the future of the ET system more generally. What should those of us concerned with workers' access to justice wish for? A shopping list would have to include the abolition of fees. However, as I have shown in this chapter, even before the introduction of fees claimants faced often insurmountable barriers to the ET. To overcome such barriers would require resources to be targeted in the most effective way so as to prioritise access to justice. The complexity of employment law and its application should be acknowledged in the retention of the ET which should, perhaps, be recognised as what it is - a court rather than an 'informal' alternative. That would require appropriate arrangements for its administration including the preservation of an independent and highly specialised judiciary. Greater investment would be required for the purposes of providing good quality independent legal advice and representation for all those who cannot afford or access it by other means.

JUSTICE AND LEGAL REMEDIES IN EMPLOYMENT DISPUTES: ADVISER AND ADVISEE PERSPECTIVES

Eleanor Kirk[*]

Introduction

Following the examination of the legal context of employment disputes in Nicole Busby's chapter, I explore in this chapter two key questions: how do people think about the law in relation to problems at work, or disputes with their employers, and how do advisers transform or augment these notions into action or inaction in relation to employment disputes?

In the context of the proliferation of individual employment rights and changes to the nature of workplace organisation and occupational structure, Citizens Advice Bureaux are increasingly becoming providers

---

[*] Eleanor Kirk is a researcher at the University of Bristol Law School. Whilst working on the 'Employment Disputes' project she was also completing her PhD on how conflict is expressed in the contemporary workplace, how workers' grievances come to be focused on particular issues, and the role therein of collective organisation. Eleanor lives in Glasgow.

of employment advice – to the extent that they have been described as a new actor in employment relations, partly filling the void left by the decline of trade unions (Abbott, 1998). Bureaux offer information and advice regarding employment law, and assistance in enforcing the law via the employment tribunal system.

As described in Adam Sales's chapter, clients bring with them varying degrees of prior understanding and expectations which advisers seek to either validate and elaborate upon, modify or transform. Clients' notions of their employment rights are not always accurate, and as well as assisting in furthering disputes, advisers may sometimes also close them down. In the context of recent changes to employment law, such as the weakening of unfair dismissal protection and the imposition of fees for tribunals, advisers are increasingly the bearers of bad news to their clients regarding available legal options. I consider in this chapter the sometimes divergent perspectives of clients and advisers regarding justice and legal remedies, and how advisers seek to manage expectations.

Laypeople and legal consciousness in employment disputes

Generally clients arrive at CABx possessing a rudimentary understanding of: their rights, how these rights apply to their situation, the legal remedies available and how these remedies might be accessed. However, some clients in our study were, prior to their disputes, unaware of the existence of the Citizens Advice service or of the possibility of challenging their employer at all. Muriel was informed of these facts through a chance meeting on an aeroplane with an Acas employee. Others came to CABx with debt or benefits problems, unaware that they might dispute employers' behaviour in relation to their troubles. Jimmy came to a CAB for advice about benefits when his employer, who owed him several months' wages, laid him off. An adviser noted that he could pursue the wages legally and made him an appointment with an employment specialist. Kim came for help with housing when her home was damaged in a fire. The housing problem and health complications had caused her problems at work which she had not sought advice about until an adviser unearthed the issues.

As Emily Rose describes in her chapter, when arriving for their first interview at the bureau, lacking knowledge of appropriate timelines, legally relevant starting points or facts, clients often relate their problems to advisers in a rather jumbled fashion. After eliciting the narrative in an orderly way, advisers translate the situation for the client, laying out relevant options. From this point, advice involves helping clients weigh up the pros and cons of particular courses of action. In rationalising their decisions, clients related their notions of justice and legality, which sometimes conflicted with advisers' recommendations about the nature of employment law, and how the Employment Tribunal System operates.

'It must be illegal'

Most clients can be observed to operate on the basis of 'natural justice' principles; they adopt a position in which egregious experiences '*must be* illegal' and seek advice regarding the validity of this supposition. Clients had often discussed the issues with other laypeople for confirmation of their sense of injustice, however vague, or the idea that 'something' could be done, and that by extension that there 'must be something that can be done *legally*' about the problem.

Before Peter came to CAB, he and his wife knew little about tribunals and what they entailed but were convinced his employer's treatment of him was illegal. Peter's wife commented:

> 'I've heard of unfair dismissal and knew it could be taken to some kind of court, but we only really got to know about them from [solicitor] ... I think that common sense would say that disabled people are protected, that they have to be. I didn't know that much about it, I just knew that there was things in place to protect you.'

Understanding of terms for types of claims such as 'unfair dismissal' or 'discrimination', or how they apply to their particular situation, was limited; many clients struggled to understand these terms, even after having them explained across several advice appointments.

In deliberating upon the pursuit of legal action, participants expressed multifaceted notions of justice: they wished to clear their name, to stop the employer from mistreating others or generally for them to 'mend their ways'. These were often contrasted with the loyalty they felt that they have shown to the employer. Once in the Employment Tribunal System, disputes tend to become focused upon financial compensation. However, the sentiment that 'it's not about the money' was ubiquitous, with clients regarding their disputes as concerning matters of principle, and looking to ETs as external authorities that might recognise the wrongs they have suffered, that their employer broke the law, and subsidiary branches of these themes: "I don't care about the money, we just want to see justice getting done" (Muriel).

Mike felt that his former employer had treated him badly and although he was struggling to find another job, "it wasn't about the money it was about proving, that they [the employer] were wrong". Many felt they were dismissed far too easily, especially where they had provided dutiful service to the employer over many years. For those who felt they could not go back to their jobs, they tended to want to have the unfairness of their situation recognised by an independent authority. Amanda felt she was dismissed unfairly after 27 years: "I said it all along. I wouldn't have cared how much of an award I got, just as long as I got the decision. That's what was most important to me."

Many wanted to 'clear their names', and being called a liar by their employer in the course of the dispute had been a sticking-point for them, a personal attack or character assassination that they could not accept. Sally "wasn't getting made out to be a liar". She:

'was wantin' to do unfair dismissal … wasn't really interested in the money, ah just wanted tae clear ma name, and [the solicitor] had sat and he spoke tae me and he said that there would need tae be some sort of figure, so we had kind of worked out between us how much ah had lost in wages.'

Disputes involving unpaid wages were clearly 'about the money', but even here, there was a symbolic quality to making employers 'pay for their crimes'. Cheryl was owed around £400:

'It was more just wanting the money back in principle … [I'd] earned it, so I should have it. Even if it was hundred pound or a thousand pound … I worked hard in there – it was long hours, short breaks, really stressful work – I thought I'm not going to let this lie, cause it's money I deserve to get.'

Whilst there was an obvious financial component to Mary's grievance she was "no' carin' too much about the money, Ah would just like tae see them gettin' paid back for what they've done … A bit of justice". Most participants were uncomfortable putting a price on their suffering. Mulling over the issue of a financial settlement in relation to her dismissal, Sarah's husband said, "it's completely out of principle so it's silly to come out with a figure … it's the winning that matters, if [Sarah] win[s] and get[s] £50, that's fine".

To many clients, 'justice' only appeared to be possible through formal legal action, even a full tribunal hearing in some cases, whereas accepting a settlement might let employers pay their way out of disputes, enabling them to continue to treat people poorly. Desiring formal justice in this way, as it takes up the time and resources of tribunals and courts, tends to be viewed pejoratively within the dominant policy rhetoric However, from the perspective of many CABx clients, this is their only realistic opportunity for a 'fair' hearing. In contrast to what they had experienced in the workplace, here it is imagined that the employer's decision making will be fully placed under scrutiny.

The fallibility of folk knowledge

Of course, lay understandings of employment law are not always correct. Some clients arrived at the Citizens Advice Bureau only after being alerted to the possibility of enforcing their rights by friends, family or chance meetings with informed individuals. While in many cases clients underestimated the scope of employment law, in others clients had higher expectations of legal protections than are warranted in reality. Correspondingly, clients are sometimes pleasantly surprised that they have legal options for redress, but advisers are often (and increasingly) the bearers of bad news to clients in terms of available legal remedies and the difficulties enforcing them. Advisers manage the expectations (and emotions) of clients who may have legitimate grievances against their employers which are likely to be only partially redressed in the uncertain event of a successful claim to tribunal. The recent weakening of employment rights (such as unfair dismissal protection) and imposition of fees for ETs as well as cuts to legal aid, and local council funding which affects CABx resources, means that there may be little positive advice to offer:

'With the cuts, you know, we get the brunt of it … we're the messenger [that] gets shot.' (CAB manager)

One adviser, discussing fees in particular felt constrained in how she could help clients:

'You're meeting people and you can't help … "I've been dismissed when I'm pregnant", "I've been dismissed because of my disability", and basically there's very little that you can do … you almost feel a bit de-skilled … you're not doing what you want to do, or what you feel you should be doing.' (CAB solicitor)

These and other quotes highlight the significant tensions in practising advice during a period in which the options for legal redress are increasingly distant:

> 'The tears in people's eyes when you tell them that the law is no good to them ... "But that's not fair". You're darn right it's not! ... a lot of my conversations to do with employment law are negative ... it's not my job to mislead people, so you have to tell them what the hurdles are going to be. But then how do you do that without talking people out of taking the case that they might win?' (Generalist adviser)

A CAB manager explained that because for many clients fees had put ETs "outwith their reach", advisers were faced with constantly disappointing clients (whose lives were often in turmoil) with the news that there is little they can do, and this impacts on CABx's ability to retain volunteers in particular:

> 'The challenge is keeping people happy to continue volunteering. When you're spending your day delivering bad news ... You can't help them, there isn't a happy outcome ... I've got to manage that with people who are coming in here you know to try and make sure they come back and they don't feel completely disheartened by it all.' (CAB manager)

Even where cases are deemed to be strong, advisers may also have to frustrate clients' expectations about the availability of free legal representation or legal aid. However much clients think they need or should have representation at an Employment Tribunal, CABx rarely have the resources to provide this assistance themselves or are able to locate reliable providers to whom they can refer clients.

Unfair but not illegal

Many clients (and some advisers) referred to the limited protection of the framework of employment rights as unjust. Cases that did not progress to the Employment Tribunal often involved circumstances that, while being highly unfair, were either not strictly illegal or difficult to provide evidence for.

Some clients, like Jack, felt they had been treated poorly, but were not qualified for legal protection. Jack had been working as a scaffolder with an employer for ten months when he had an argument with a colleague at work and lost his temper. He was trying to preserve health and safety standards, but he was nevertheless dismissed. Jack came to the Citizens Advice Bureau after discussing his situation with a friend who told him that his employer could not just sack him on a whim without any warning or investigation of the alleged misdemeanour. The friend told him, "they've got to give you a warning or it's unfair dismissal". He initially told the friend that he was just going to leave it but the friend had told him, "you should do them for that". Jack was unaware that there was a two year qualifying period of service for unfair dismissal but suspected that his employer could not just dismiss him so easily. He learned about the Employment Tribunal system at the Citizens Advice Bureau. However, as he was not qualified for unfair dismissal protection, an adviser told Jack that the best outcome he will likely achieve is to obtain a weeks' notice pay. He was surprised and disappointed, asking, "is that all?!" After learning this, Jack was not sure that pursuing the dispute was worth the hassle, even though he was having financial difficulties, being out of work, on benefits and in debt. He did not return to the bureau.

Bullying by management is a common grievance brought to CAB, but not one that is well protected by law. Advisers often sympathised but had to inform clients that bringing a successful claim of this type to tribunal is very difficult:

'There's nothing you can do about that, it seems, it wouldn't stand up ... bullying and harassment, from what I heard, it seems really hard ... I've seen a lot of general "picking on me" stuff that really upsets people. "He shouldn't be allowed to do that". ... and it sounds awful, and then I've got to turn it to people and say, "look, employment law is ... [limited]". (Volunteer generalist adviser)

In such circumstances, advisers can only legitimately encourage clients to raise those aspects of their complaints which are demonstrable and clearly covered by legal jurisdictions:

"'Have you had any unpaid wages? Or are you being paid the minimum wage? ... These are the things you can claim for here. Have you got anything that fits into these categories?" ... there's nothing you can really do for being just picked on.' (Volunteer generalist adviser)

Advisers were circumspect in suggesting clients might bring claims of certain types such as constructive dismissal, which involve leaving a job to pursue a very uncertain outcome at tribunal; this option was considered as particularly risky given current labour market conditions. A CAB solicitor told Lesley, a teacher who wanted to leave her job because of bullying, that "as difficult as it is I wouldn't advise you to quit. You're employed and being paid and it might be difficult to find another job just now".

Advisers may also have to close down disputes if the time limits set by the Employment Tribunal process have been passed. Gordon wished to dispute the terms of his redeployment following a redundancy situation and was awaiting an appointment with a CAB solicitor. However, there was a mix-up regarding Gordon's appointment date and when he turned up at the CAB, he was informed that he had missed his slot with their solicitor. By the time the client saw the solicitor, he had missed the deadline to dispute his redeployment. The solicitor told Gordon that were it not for the time bar, he would have had a strong case. Gordon was bewildered and responded that his original position was not genuinely redundant as someone else is doing it. The solicitor cut him off saying, "I understand what is being done, but after four weeks, the door closes", after which point Gordon could not claim unfair dismissal and does not get a redundancy payment. Gordon was livid that the opportunity to dispute his treatment was snatched away from him.

Even where clients are deemed to have strong legal cases, advisers often suggest that they may have to lower their expectations of the 'justice' they will obtain via the ETS. If successful, an ET might result in some compensation, but rarely would anyone 'get the truth' or 'clear their name' in the way clients commonly desired. Amanda and Sarah were jointly bringing unfair dismissal claims against their former employer. An adviser checked at one point whether they might consider re-engagement. Amanda replied "No ... I'm 99% sure that they'd just make up some new reason to make me redundant or get me out." Nevertheless, "I said it all along. I wouldn't have cared how much of an award I got, just as long as I got the decision. That's what was most important to me." Sarah's response to the same question was that she could not go back but "just want[s] them to deal with people properly", and change the way "[the boss] speaks to people!" The adviser's response to Sarah was similar to the one she gave to Amanda, "the tribunal will not be concerned with getting an apology or changing practices. They might not give you the remedy you want in that respect".

Following advice at CAB that the type of justice ETs provide may not match their expectations, generally clients were pragmatic about modifying, or monetarising their sense of recompense. Many were nevertheless reluctant to agree to financial settlements that would allow employers to avoid hearings, or impose confidentiality agreements, meaning outcomes such as exposing their employers, clearing their name and having their 'day in court' would be forfeited. However, often clients are worn down and heed the advice that proceeding to a full hearing is guaranteed to be a continuing struggle for uncertain gain. Peter's former employer offered what he considered to be a derisory payment as part of a settlement agreement in an unfair dismissal claim, on the proviso that he signed a confidentiality clause. The couple were uncertain about paying the full hearing fee and decided to settle at this point. Peter's wife reflected:

> 'It was signing documents never to discuss it. I would rather that they just kept their money and walked away from it. It was never about the money. It was about the way that they made Peter feel ... We just wanted them tae be made aware that they had done wrong.'

The parameters of settlement also conflicted with Muriel's desire for justice, exposing the employer for what they had done:

> 'People were saying to me, "don't take the money ... just go to court ... you won't be able to say what the truth is so basically they're just going to buy your silence".'

The CAB solicitor representing her attempted to manage Muriel's expectations about potential remedies, saying during an advice appointment:

> 'A lot of people say to me, "I want to clear my name". However, an employment tribunal is not looking at whether you did something wrong or not but really whether the employer did something wrong in relation to your employment. But the employee's record does not change.' (CAB solicitor)

Muriel continued to view her dispute in broader terms of right and wrong, despite the solicitor's advice:

> 'He said to me, "oh you might never find out the truth and you might", but at the same time I've got to try ... I could have just walked away and just left it ... I've moved on with my life now but at the same time you can't really get closure until you really find out.'

However, following the breakdown of her relationship with her partner, Muriel decided to accept a settlement facilitated through Acas and her solicitor, having lost the will to fight.

Ray was adamant that he wanted reinstatement after being dismissed, and would not accept a financial settlement, against the advice of his CAB representative:

'They offered me £2000 to drop [the claim] … I says, "I don't want money I'm not after money. I really want ma job back and I want them tae find oot why they actually sacked me".'

Ray was unsuccessful at hearing and walked away with nothing. However, when asked whether he ever regretted not settling, he said: "No, no, because I thought the way they went about it was totally wrong and I thought 20 years working in the same place and just to be dismissed like that."

Sometimes what an adviser may view as the 'best' outcome may not fit with a client's notion of justice. However, advisers are only offering guidance on the likely remedies available in the ETS which may not offer the kind of 'justice' many clients seek.

Conclusion

The employment tribunal system in the UK involves a passive-reactive system which relies upon a high level of capability and knowledge among individuals in order that they can understand and enforce their rights (Dickens, 2012), rather than proactivity on the part of employers to meet agreed standards. Yet our research shows that employees presenting to Citizens Advice Bureaux hold only vague notions of employment law, often drawing upon a natural sense of (in)justice in which what appears to them as immoral *must be* illegal.

Not all bureaux are able to either train or recruit the level of expertise required to provide employment advice or representation. A recent survey of CABx in Scotland found that 50% described themselves as providing specialist employment advice (Wood and Rose,

2014). Where specialist employment advice is available, advisers are increasingly the bearers of bad news to clients regarding the extent of their rights, regarding the cost and difficulty of bringing a claim (particularly post-fees), regarding the availability of representation on a day-to-day basis and in front of employment tribunals, and regarding the remedies available and likelihood of receiving any eventual award. Many conversations are 'negative', as one adviser put it, adding to the difficulty and emotional management required in advice giving. For bureaux managers, the challenge is to recruit and retain volunteers who may find that a good proportion of their work involves delivering bad news to many clients regarding their prospects for resolving a work-related grievance via the Employment Tribunal system. It is perhaps unsurprising given this experience that as organisations, Citizens Advice and Citizens Advice Scotland has been campaigning for an alternative to the employment tribunal system as a means of enforcing employment rights, looking to state enforcement through some form of 'employment commission' (see CAS, 2014).

6

PRECARITY AND 'AUSTERITY': EMPLOYMENT DISPUTES AND INEQUALITIES

Adam Sales[*]

Introduction

The Citizens Advice service expanded in the post-war period in the UK, and reflected economic, political and social settlements of the time, not least those between capital, labour and government about the conditions of employment. Since the late 1970s, those settlements have been dissolved; the power balance between labour and capital has tilted dramatically in favour of employers, and work has become more contingent and precarious. Employment is increasingly characterised by non-standard, flexible, temporary and insecure working arrangements. This process of casualisation, which Bourdieu (2010: 151) calls 'flexploitation', involves 'insecurity inducing strategies' which

---

[*] Adam Sales is a sociologist who has carried out previous research exploring power inequalities in relation to health, education and law, using the thinking of Pierre Bourdieu. He was a Research Associate on the 'Citizens Advice Bureaux and Employment Disputes' project.

105

exploit the growing vulnerability of workers and those looking for work, forcing them into more intense competition with each other, and therefore acceptance of their own subordination. Workers are not prepared or able, individually or collectively, to challenge their employer and their working conditions, so uncertain are they about their future job prospects.

A variety of legal and social protections have been withdrawn in the name of freeing markets and enterprise from unnecessary constraints – these protections included welfare benefits, employment law, trades union rights and forms of legal redress (as described by Nicole Busby in Chapter Four). The period of 'austerity' has seen the further erosion of social and legal protections and a deepening of precarity, representing the loss of a 'bargain of trust or security' between worker, employer and state (Standing, 2011: 8). The increasing deregulation of the labour market and its contracts, the loss and individualisation of workers' rights, and the shrinking of collective protection provided by unions are leading more workers to come to the Citizens Advice service to deal with their employment problems and to find possible lines of redress. Citizens Advice thus finds itself in dramatically changed circumstances, as Morag McDermont argues in Chapter One, with shrinking capacities encountering rising need. This encounter between growing need and shrinking resources creates new barriers to justice.

Our research into CAB clients' experience of employment disputes revealed that a high proportion of them were working in precarious conditions. Contemporary employment disputes provide powerful illustrations of the new conditions of precarity: working lives that are characterised by vulnerability, uncertainty and insecurity. Such disputes centre on the breakdown of relationships between workers and employers that take place in a context of a dramatically changing balance of power between workers and employers (Pollert, 2010). The combination of powerlessness, insecurity and institutional isolation was a central dynamic of the experiences of many of the workers in our research.

As Eleanor Kirk's chapter reveals, workers often do not know their rights relating to their employment issue. Yet what is also key is the extent to which they lack certain resources through which they might be able to deal with their dispute, namely the educational background enabling individuals to understand relevant employment law; the formal or informal social networks through which this information might be shared and discussed; or the financial capital to pay for professional legal advice. Most workers felt that the CAB was the only source of advice or help available to them; "there was no one else to go to" was the most common reason for attending. As one participant described this situation, "the thing is I don't know all the law or anything; I don't know where to go, what is the next step".

"Little or nothing you can do" – "They can do what they want"

Workers often believed that the law protected them more than it actually did. Their perception was that their employer was doing or had done something wrong; these perceptions however were not commonly informed by a good knowledge of employment law, legal procedures or employment rights. One employment adviser commented: "Very often, people think 'it's not fair' in the universal natural justice sense of not being fair." CAB advisers commonly talked about managing clients' 'unrealistic' expectations. Sometimes the advice was that there was little that could be done, with few options for formal legal redress. Workers were advised in these cases to 'let it go'. For some of these workers their employer had acted unfairly but within the first two years of their employment, thereby blocking access to a tribunal for unfair dismissal.

A cleaner taking part in our research had been working for almost a year and a half for a company when she was dismissed after being verbally abused by her manager. A few months before the incident, the company she worked for had been transferred to another company and the problems seem to have arisen then. Similarly, an office administrator had no access to legal redress after being dismissed even though her GP authorised a period of sick leave for clinical depression. As her adviser, a CAB employment solicitor, put it:

'Basically the government have given them two years to get rid of you, if they don't want you. It hasn't got better for employees … So the fairness of it does not come into it; you can't do anything about it.'

Uncertain futures

Insecurity created through uncertainty about future employment prospects profoundly affected workers' feelings and courses of action, including the advice they received. Workers were often concerned about the negative impact of the reference their employer would write for them. A hotel worker was unfairly dismissed within two years and had been told in her Gateway session to write a letter of grievance. But at her advice appointment, the adviser pointed out the practical limitations of this course of action, and the threat to her next job if this was done:

'So the letter is getting things off your chest; it is not achieving anything. If you want to get another job, you might need to think about not doing anything, put it to one side, as a bad experience, and forget about it.'

The threat of dismissal or concern over future job prospects hung over vulnerable workers, preventing them from challenging employers individually or collectively, leading to 'a crushing censorship that forbids mobilization and takes away bargaining power' (Bourdieu, 2010: 156). As one of our participants noted,

'the other people who are working in the same situation like me from different countries, they will be very quiet because they are thinking that they will lose their job if they will start to speak because I am this example now for them.'

Ignored by employers

Workers often talked about being unable to contact their employer to discuss their dispute. Whether or not it was an intentional strategy on the part of employers, we observed the extent to which their proving elusive for employees exploited workers' lack of status and ability to interact with them. Thus one of our participants, who spoke no English, visited the CAB after having worked for three months for an agency without being paid. Her husband, who spoke some English, had been trying to speak to the agency on the phone but had been repeatedly fobbed off.

Another agency worker had been suspended pending an investigation by the company he was working for and failed to get any response from his agency when he tried to find out what was happening. The CAB adviser had noted that the point of contact with the agency was "a person who is of limited authority", which the adviser's colleague felt was a deliberate stalling tactic on the part of the employer – a common strategy in our research. The adviser felt the case was "very difficult to make progress on ... they [the agency] don't want to prejudice their contract [with the company the worker was working for]".

Institutional intervention – "it goes to high quarters"

CAB advisers would often send out grievance letters to employers. Workers who had tried to communicate with employers but failed felt that communication from an official third party could make a difference (the tendency among advisers, it should be noted, was to draft these letters in the worker's name, believing that their direct intervention might be counterproductive). Thus a cleaner who had been waiting for three months to receive some unpaid holiday pay was hopeful when the CAB adviser offered to write a letter to his employer. He put faith in the official authority of the CAB to make a difference:

'Yeah better, because she's a bureau … if they're writing letter, […] because I can't write the official letter […] if you speak to someone it's different from bureau … it goes [to] high quarters.'

An agency HGV driver who was asked why he was pleased that the CAB were writing to his employer, replied, "because I ask [the employer] three times to make it proper, and they just ignore me". In one case a shop worker had been helped in drafting an email to her employer, and felt that the expertise and technical knowledge of the adviser had made a difference:

'If I'd sent my email to my employer that would not have had the same effect. He would not have accepted that it was redundancy. But because the adviser wrote that in such a way, it had an argument to it, so it made them think, because it was a professional argument … I don't know about these things.'

Early 'pre-legal' intervention – offsetting power inequalities

One CAB in our research had pioneered a strategy of early 'pre-legal' intervention in employment disputes, something that had proved to be very successful. The leader of the newly trained volunteer employment advice team described having "a light bulb moment" in which he realised that, as trained advisers, the team all possessed the considerable skills of negotiation required to communicate with the employer directly.

'Everybody here should be a good negotiator with third parties … […] Nobody thinks twice about ringing up the Council Tax office and arguing, or the bailiffs, doing a deal, or a landlord, so why is an employer so different? You know, we've got the negotiation skills. There's just been this phobia about "better not call employers, we might make it worse".'

Armed with sufficient knowledge of employment rights and law, advisers would now place greater emphasis upon attempting to informally negotiate with the employer without formal recourse to law:

> 'We say, "Citizens Advice here, we've got one of your employees in the bureau right now. There's an issue, which I'm not sure you're aware about to do with unpaid wages – all this chap wants to do is get this sorted out. Is there anything we can do today to get that fixed?" And that kind of informal approach rather than even starting a grievance process can work, because the client leaves the room, the employer's sorted out, the client's sorted out, the relationship isn't damaged, and it hasn't taken an awful lot of time.'

It is through this 'pre-legal' work that the importance of services like the CAB is made starkly apparent. With substantial barriers existing for access to formal justice, and precarious employment increasingly becoming the norm, an employment advice approach focused upon informal tactics of intervention can potentially offset some of the power inequalities between employer and worker and the increasing exploitation of the worker's labour.

PART THREE
INTRODUCTION

John Clarke and Samuel Kirwan

Thus far we have stayed within advice on its own terms, exploring how it is organised, interpreted and challenged. We move now to a set of broader questions: what can advice tell us about the society we live in and about the experience and interpretation of the laws that shape it? What are the different ways in which advice practices change lives beyond the direct effects of the advice itself? In these final reflections we start to address the broader life of advice.

Part Three begins with the experiences of Brian, an unrepresented claimant at Employment Tribunal who received help from a CAB at various stages in this process, describing the difficulty for individuals of understanding the range of legal concepts at play and navigating a complex and dispiriting system. This is followed by a reflection by Joe McGlade, a vastly experienced adviser based in Northern Ireland, who gives an adviser's perspective on the emotional and procedural difficulties faced by Brian and the possibilities for reforming this system in favour of vulnerable clients.

Chapter Seven explores the interplay between power and legality in the processes of advice work, drawing on users' experiences of these processes. Chapter Eight offers an analysis of how the issues faced by clients, experienced as deeply personal matters, are turned into matters of law, while Chapter Nine explores the shifting boundaries separating law and life in the work of debt advice. Chapter Ten reflects back on the changing place, possibilities and problems of Citizens Advice in the context of 'austerity' – a time when citizenship itself is called into question.

These chapters explore the unseen dynamics and effects of advice practice, bringing together the advice interview and its emotional dynamics with the social dynamics that both clients and advisers bring to the table. Two key questions run through these observations. The first is the importance of narrative: how the stories we tell about our problems shape those problems, and the task for the adviser of shaping the very different stories told by law into this framework. The second concerns *power*. What power runs through law, and is it only available to those who understand or are able to play with legal concepts? What power do advisers, as people acting *within* law, have to change or frame it? Are they simply actors within law, or something else?

This final part leads us also to consider the future of advice: what role will advice play in the considerable changes to come? While an event that holds wide-ranging implications for the future of law and citizenship – the EU referendum – occurred after our project was concluded, these chapters provide an indication of how advice might inform what course we as a society are to map through this changing terrain.

CASE STUDY THREE
'BRIAN': AN UNREPRESENTED CLAIMANT

Case study compiled by Eleanor Kirk

Brian had help from a CAB solicitor preparing his claim of constructive dismissal against his employer. However, having to represent himself at hearing was an enormous strain, especially given his limited education, severe dyslexia and the stress he was already suffering as a result of the nature of the dispute.

The story

Brian, a man in his early 40s, had worked as a car valet in a car sales yard for more than eight years. During this time, he claimed to have experienced verbal abuse from his immediate manager, the son of the owner. Brian had talked with the owner about the abuse on a number of occasions. This would improve the situation temporarily, but the bullying would resume shortly thereafter. When Brian attended a hospital appointment his manager phoned him, swearing at him and demanding he return to work. Brian collapsed shortly afterwards and was advised by a nurse not to go back to work. Brian resigned from his job. Initially Brian did not intend to seek legal redress for the way he had been treated at work and began looking for new work.

After some reflection, Brian felt that his boss should not be able to get away with forcing him to leave a job that he loved. His wife encouraged Brian to contact Acas, whose representative suggested that he see a solicitor. Brian attended a free initial appointment with a solicitor who told him to submit a grievance letter to his employer and that further free legal information could be obtained from a solicitor at the CAB. Brian had a Gateway interview. He then received a phone call from the employment solicitor at the CAB, who advised him that he needed to wait for a few more weeks before he would be eligible for legal aid, following the loss of his employment. An appointment was then made with the CAB employment solicitor who formally assessed his eligibility for legal aid. Brian was deemed eligible and although he had been nervous about meeting with the solicitor, when it became clear that they were going to take the steps required to progress the claim, he was very happy for her to act on his behalf. Brian was not confident about his ability to communicate effectively in written form, in large part because he is dyslexic. Brian referred to having the assistance of the solicitor as being like a "weight lifting". Previously Brian had felt "on me own" and like "the walls were coming in on me".

The solicitor took a detailed account of Brian's employment problem, teasing out initial evidence and legal arguments for *constructive dismissal*, a term Brian had heard from speaking with the first solicitor, but referred to as 'compulsive dismissal' during the appointment at the CABx. The solicitor tried to explain this term, the legal argument required and the general procedures involved in submitting a claim and the legal course of action after that.

When the employer ignored a grievance letter, the solicitor submitted an ET1 form and helped Brian to prepare for his ET hearing. She was not able to represent him at hearing, as legal aid funding would not cover this. The solicitor reassured Brian that judges liked it when a party spoke on their own behalf, but the thought that his employer might be represented by a solicitor filled Brian with dread:

'So, where his solicitor's going to have these big fancy words and that, I'm going to come out like Mr Joe Bloggs, know what I mean? Who are courts going to listen to?'

The solicitor had prepared some questions for the participant to use but suggested that Brian think of others that he wanted to ask. Brian did not feel confident in this task, but worked with his sister, who was better educated, to prepare these. When reviewed by the CAB solicitor, it became apparent that many were more statements rather than questions or were otherwise inappropriate. The solicitor attempted to prepare the participant for the tribunal by explaining the order of proceedings, how to manage his 'bundles' and whom to ask to read out his witness statement, as the participant did not want to do this himself because of his dyslexia. The participant sought clarification on whether he was the claimant or the respondent, not knowing these terms.

Brian was extremely nervous at the hearing. He did not know which documents to hand over to the clerk or how to arrange for the judge to read out his witness statement (as he is dyslexic). Brian did not always understand the questions asked by the judge, nor was he able to provide a detailed account of the verbal abuse he experienced. The employer also represented himself. He was also not always able to follow the protocols required of the tribunal and took an aggressive approach throughout. In his cross-examination of his ex-boss, Brian simply read out the questions which the CAB solicitor had prepared for him. He did not ask further questions when the respondent replied, or interrogate anything he said. In the summing up stage, the respondent, more articulate than Brian, put forward his case against Brian. Exhausted and intimidated, Brian said only a little when the judge asked him if he had anything more to say in summing up his case.

Nevertheless, Brian won his case and was called upon to attend a remedy hearing. The CAB solicitor helped to prepare him for this. In this hearing, the accounts Brian provided for a new business that he had set up were questioned by the employer. The judge awarded Brian £8300, just over half of the amount claimed in his schedule of loss, being persuaded by some of the arguments by the employer challenging Brian's business accounts.

The employer did not pay up immediately. After the hearing, Brian and his wife were verbally abused and physically threated by his former boss. Brian went to the police and they visited the respondent, threatening him with an injunction. Brian's car was also vandalised twice. He felt that the employer was "just trying to bully me to drop it all. I don't know. I've had enough". Eventually, Brian got help from the CAB solicitor to utilise the fast track tribunal award enforcement scheme. Technically, legal aid does not cover assistance with the enforcement of awards but the solicitor helped because Brian simply would not have been able to do it himself. A bailiff was sent to the respondents' car sales site and was threatened verbally and physically by the respondent, to such an extent that the police were again involved. With the threat of having some of his stock taken to pay for the award, the respondent wrote a cheque.

A REFLECTION ON CASE STUDY THREE: 'BRIAN'

Joe McGlade[*]

The difficulties involved in constructive dismissal claims

Constructive dismissal claims are amongst the most difficult types of cases to take to an Employment Tribunal. Such cases require high levels of knowledge; employment advisers will often argue amongst themselves about constructive dismissal cases. A substantial difficulty with any employment case is being able to secure supporting evidence. It is very rare in ET cases that someone walks in with comprehensive and complete evidence; and how do you get witnesses, people who are willing to stand up and testify against their own employer?

Constructive dismissal cases are also extremely painful for the claimant. We often find people folding at an early stage because of the stress of taking a case. On the Citizens Advice information system

[*] Having worked in various jobs, on returning to Northern Ireland in 2001 Joe McGlade volunteered with Citizens Advice, where he has been a Generalist Adviser and Tribunal Representative for 15 years. He holds specialisms in anti-discrimination and employment law casework. Here Joe reflects upon Brian's case study as both the holder of a law degree and as an adviser with many years' experience of dealing with clients' employment disputes.

there are big red warning triangles to emphasise the difficulties inherent in advancing a constructive dismissal case.

Firstly, the claimant needs to understand what the term 'constructive dismissal' actually means. To successfully argue that s/he has been constructively dismissed, a claimant will have to show a fundamental breach of one of the 'express' or 'implied' terms in the contract. To effectively proceed, Brian would have needed to understand the written terms of his contract of employment. These would form the basis of the 'express' terms of his contract. (Whilst there was an obligation on Brian's employer to provide a written statement of the main terms and conditions of his employment, we cannot tell from the case study if he ever received these.) This creates a major obstacle for any unrepresented claimant and this obstacle becomes all the more daunting considering that Brian was severely dyslexic. If Brian had not had an experienced solicitor at the CAB to prepare his case I doubt he would have proceeded to a tribunal hearing.

Starting the advice chain

Following his resignation, and with the support of his wife, Brian sought advice from Acas. At this point, the chain of advice began, with Acas suggesting he seek a solicitor's advice. He attended a free initial appointment with a solicitor. This begs the questions: if Brian had been a single person, and/or had not his wife been aware of the Acas service, and/or if the initial interview with the solicitor had cost him money, and/or if free advice had not been available via legal aid, would he have taken the crucial early steps he managed to take?

Brian is both vulnerable and unlikely to be able to navigate the system on his own. He was extremely lucky: his wife being aware of Acas, the timely intervention by Acas, the fact that the CAB had a solicitor – this was a postcode lottery, but luck should not be involved in providing for legal need. Brian felt a "weight lifting" when he knew he was not fighting his case alone.

Knowing your enemy

When advancing a client's claim via the Employment Tribunal system, it is often useful to attempt to ascertain the likely mindset of the respondent (the employer), and to attempt to predict the respondent's likely response to actions taken by the client, or by his or her representative – knowing your enemy, so to speak. Thus, had I been advising Brian on his case, I would have asked detailed questions relating to the personalities involved in the management of his employer's business. The answers to such questions would influence the tactical direction of the case. Hypothetical scenarios may help to emphasise the point of such questions.

Scenario 1: Brian informs me that his employer has a well-structured business, with a full-time HR presence and clear and effective lines of communication between management and employees. Brian attends monthly staff meetings, and has regular formal supervision, backed up by yearly appraisal. Brian's employer has a clear and robust anti-bullying policy, and Brian is aware of staff being dismissed for bullying previously.

In this scenario, the existence of coherent structures within the employer's business would substantially enhance Brian's chances of resolving his problems at an early stage, thereby serving to preserve as much goodwill as possible. In such a scenario, and time permitting, I would suggest that Brian seek to resolve his problems as informally as the circumstances will allow. If such approaches prove ineffective, I would advise Brian to escalate his approaches to his employer gradually. In this scenario, I believe it likely that the matters complained of could be effectively remedied without the need to issue proceedings.

Scenario 2: Brian informs me that his employer's business is controlled very tightly by two people, a father and a son. There are no structures or policies in place, so far as Brian is aware. When starting work, and to date, Brian did not receive any paperwork whatsoever, and he does not receive supervision or appraisal. Both father and son are verbally aggressive and confrontational. They do not believe they need to spend time or money on HR advice.

In this scenario, as no effective internal structures exist, it is highly unlikely that Brian's case would be resolved at an early stage. Any attempt by Brian to do so would likely lead to summary dismissal. In this scenario, therefore, if Brian intends to achieve justice, he would need to be prepared to issue proceedings and advance the case to full hearing.

In my experience, knowledge that an employer will approach any challenge in an aggressive and emotional manner can actually prove to be an advantage to the aggrieved employee. Often, aggrieved employees approach Citizens Advice with stories of mistreatment in the workplace, but with no evidence whatsoever. With the specific intention of generating evidence, we may send a polite letter to the employer. We may then receive, by return, a three-page rant which substantiates our client's case!

In Brian's case, it is noted that his immediate manager, and the main actor against him, is the son of the owner of the business. As Brian's only option was to speak directly to the owner of the business in the hope of rectifying the situation, it seems likely that there was nobody within the organisation who worked in a HR capacity – indeed, most small employers do not have any HR capacity. Where there is no HR presence in a company there could be no dispassionate evaluation of what happened to Brian. At Citizens Advice we have dealt with cases where HR have been able to effectively intervene to resolve problems similar to those experienced by Brian.

The limitations of a company's internal processes

When Brian informed the owner about what was happening to him, he was informing his employer of unacceptable activity and behaviour in the employer's workplace. From that point in time, due to his obligations under health and safety law, and due to his obligations towards his employee under employment law, it was incumbent upon the employer to act effectively. This did not happen.

I suggest there may be a number of reasons why Brian's approach to his employer proved ineffectual. It may be that the employer was ignorant of his obligations under health and safety and employment law. It may be that, while aware of his obligations in these regards, the employer deliberately chose to ignore such obligations. If the employer chose to deliberately ignore his obligations, it is possible that he understood the value to him of the imbalance in power between himself and Brian, and thus proceeded on the assumption that either Brian would not act, or, if he did, the difficulties inherent in progressing a claim via the Employment Tribunal system would work in his interests, and contrary to Brian's.

Whatever the truth of the matter, I think it is fair to assume that, as the person complained about was the employer's son, it was highly unlikely that the employer approached the matter in an objective and neutral matter, as he is required to do. As there was no effective HR presence, there was no opportunity for Brian's issues to be dispassionately resolved at an early stage.

The emotional damage of abuse and bullying

The manager's actions towards Brian are described as 'abuse' and 'bullying'. These terms are quite emotive, and describe actions far removed from simple differences of opinion or viewpoint as to how the relationship between Brian and his employer was operating or otherwise. From the case study, it appears that Brian's manager did not like him.

It is my experience that, where a client is seeking advice on breach of an implied term, such as breach of trust and confidence, the client would often feel that the experience has caused them emotional damage. In the case study, Brian had worked for his employer for more than eight years. I would assume that, over the years of working profitably for the employer, Brian thought that, if a problem arose, the years of loyal service he had given would stand him in good stead. I would suspect, further, that when Brian discovered that his trust and confidence was misplaced, he was devastated.

It is also my experience that, in a significant percentage of cases, the emotional damage sustained by the employee due to mistreatment in the workplace is often compounded by the stress involved in attempting to access justice via the Employment Tribunal system. It is to Brian's credit that he managed to endure the stress he was obviously experiencing, and that he was ultimately successful. Unfortunately, I would suggest that Brian's case is atypical. At Citizens Advice we regularly encounter potential claimants who decline to issue proceedings due to the stress that they anticipate they will experience. In such cases, it is often the personal characteristics of the aggrieved worker which militate against them being able to successfully navigate the Employment Tribunal process.

It is noted that, though he received excellent support from Acas and a Citizens Advice solicitor, ultimately, Brian faced the Employment Tribunal alone as a Litigant in Person. The Employment Disputes research (NSLC, 2016) shows that Litigants in Person face considerable barriers to justice when using the Employment Tribunal system. In my experience as an adviser, these barriers are faced by all unrepresented people, irrespective of their abilities or personal characteristics.

The impact of the employer as representing himself

In this case the employer also represented himself. If he had obtained representation, the outcome may well have been different. Indeed, when I read this case study I was amazed that Brian got where he did. He was unable to provide a detailed account of abuse. If the employer had had a legal representative s/he would have torn Brian apart, making him look like a liar. There was no cross-examination of the employer by Brian – here a legal representative would have won or lost the case. As the respondent did not have a lawyer Brain was not subject to threats of the employer's legal costs been awarded against him – many claimants are put off from pursuing a claim because of such a threat.

The employer did not engage in any of the dispute resolution mechanisms. It is unlikely that this was because he was stupid. More likely he thought that there was nothing that Brain would do, and the chances were that the claim would fall away without the employer doing anything – and statistically he would have been right. But in this case the CAB paperwork must have been amazing. Reading between the lines, the employer's aggressive approach probably made the judge realise that Brian's case was valid – that the employer was abusive and bullying.

The use of Alternative Dispute Resolution

Citizens Advices believe it to be imperative, in many cases, to consider Alternative Dispute Resolution (ADR) mechanisms at the earliest opportunity with a view to resolving workplace disputes in a timely fashion. We have found this approach to have a number of advantages. Successful resolution of potential claims via ADR frees the potential claimant from the rigours of the Employment Tribunal system as it currently stands, and saves the Exchequer the expense of funding such litigation. In certain cases, the use of ADR can serve to resolve disputes between employers and employees whilst preserving goodwill, thereby maximising the chances that the employee will remain in employment. Unfortunately, there are cases, such as Brian's, where ADR attempts may prove fruitless. It is likely that in Brian's case, any attempt at ADR would likely have been treated with contempt. Should his employer have so dismissed any attempt at ADR, under the current system, he could have done so without any negative consequences to his business. We believe that there is force to the argument that, in such cases, increased statutory regulation should lead to sanctions against errant employers (or employees), if it is adjudged that they acted unreasonably during an ADR process. We believe, further, that resources should be made available to organisations such as Citizens Advice to provide a comprehensive and effective ADR structure on a national basis, working in a timely fashion, and at a grassroots level.

7

POWER AND LEGALITY IN BENEFITS ADVICE

Alison Kite[*]

Since the 1990s, many Citizens Advice Bureaux have run advice sessions based in GP surgeries, in recognition of the links between poverty, poor health and the need for advice. Research has shown that such services are effective in improving benefits uptake and may also contribute to psychological health. In this chapter I broaden this focus by exploring how advice impacts on issues of powerlessness which have been shown to be central to the experience of poverty and social exclusion. I draw upon qualitative interviews which were carried out with 12 Citizens Advice clients who attended a GP-based advice service in 2012; clients were drawn from two bureaux, one based in a rural area in Wales and one in an urban area in the South West. I argue that the 'powerlessness' observed among clients as they sought to negotiate the benefits system does not imply that they are passive victims in this process, but rather individuals whose ability to take action is constrained by a lack of resources and power. I further

---

[*] Alison Kite has recently completed a PhD on the delivery of Citizens Advice services in GP surgeries. Before this she worked in the voluntary sector and in local government. She has been interested in advice work since the 1990s when she trained as a volunteer with Citizens Advice before becoming a welfare rights adviser with a local charity.

explore the key role played by the Citizens Advice service in addressing these critical imbalances.

Context

Eleven of the clients who were interviewed had long-term health problems and one was a full-time carer for his wife. All had sought advice about welfare benefits, with the majority seeking advice about disability and/or sickness benefit claims. At the time of the research, an increasing number of Citizens Advice clients were seeking advice about Employment and Support Allowance (ESA), which had replaced Incapacity Benefit and Income Support for people unable to work because of long-term health problems or disability. The new benefit introduced the Work Capability Assessment, which has been criticised by, amongst others, disability activists, Citizens Advice and the independent review process which was established to assess its implementation. Critics argue that the test is flawed, mechanistic and impersonal. Many of the interviewees' advice problems concerned ESA and the Work Capability Assessment.

Participants described a number of ways in which they felt disempowered by the problems they faced and how the advice they received helped to address this disempowerment. In the following sections I will explore the four key themes emerging from their accounts: access to information; communicating with institutions; being questioned; and gathering evidence.

Access to information

Many interviewees talked about the complexity of the benefits system and the poor level of written and verbal communication from the Department for Work and Pensions. Complaints included: finding the rules and regulations for benefits confusing and contradictory; being given partial, incorrect or conflicting information by officials; and not being told when changes to the benefits system were to be implemented. Clients experienced these problems regardless of their level of education:

> 'You know it's a bit of a minefield, … if you have this benefit it can knock this benefit, but you may be able to get this benefit, … so, just didn't know where I was like.'

> 'I thought that they were there to help me, and I thought if I had a problem they'd tell me, well you can claim for this or you can claim for that, but it doesn't work like that. They tell you the basic forms you can claim, they don't tell you about any wider … the full picture.'

Advisers helped clients by providing accurate information about the whole system, explaining what people could and could not apply for. For example, one woman said that her adviser explained "why you're able to claim for something and if you're not allowed to claim for something she'll explain why". Another said his adviser was able to tell him "there's no point going for that because you won't get it". Another emphasised that her adviser was "honest" and told her what she was entitled to and what she was not entitled to. For some, this reduced their sense of fear in their interactions with the system; their adviser helped them through the minefield.

Some interviewees highlighted the role that books played in the advice process; seeing advisers use these books appeared to give clients confidence in the advice that they received. For example, one woman explained how her adviser used "a law book, it's like this wonderful bible in a sense for them". Another woman described how her adviser's access to books on benefits meant the adviser could give her the "proper information" and compared this with the "benefit people" who "don't really give you the information". One man, who felt that benefits officials were in the dark about the latest rules and regulations, said that his adviser had "up-to-date information and knows exactly what should be happening". Another said his adviser had "the old books, the new books, all the different benefits".

One woman gave a vivid description of how she felt empowered by the information she was given by her adviser, describing Citizens Advice as her "main gun" in her benefits appeal, providing her with "bullets" of information:

'What can I say about the bullets, it's, you're armed with your information ... and then you can say well ... you're saying that, actually no, the CAB, and it's the *law*....' [Her emphasis]

Communicating with institutions: asking questions

Interviewees often experienced in their interactions with institutions the administrative problems commonly associated with bureaucracies (for example being given conflicting information by different departments). Such experiences left people feeling powerless. In these situations advisers were described as being able to step in and get to the bottom of the situation. For example, one man talking about a problem with his benefit claim, said his adviser:

'was on the phone for ages trying to just, trying to dig ... it was such a mix up and I didn't know where I'd gone wrong or where the Job Centre had gone wrong ... and you know, they did, they did a very good job on me, I was really pleased how much they'd found out.'

Some interviewees felt Citizens Advice were able to get their questions answered because advisers had more 'clout' with the institutions concerned. For example, one man said:

'These places ... try to fob you off whereas if they know Citizens Advice are involved, or any legal person, they tend to take it more seriously.'

However, he went on to describe how the knowledge he had gained through the advice process had helped him to feel more confident now in asking questions:

> 'Often I get letters now and I'll ring up the benefit place myself. I am more confident of how I can talk ... whereas before I probably would have tried to deal with it on the phone and got angry and frustrated you know what I mean ... because I know what I'm talking about, I know more of how it works, I'm able to function with asking the questions.'

Some interviewees also made a favourable comparison between their communications with Citizens Advice and those with the Department for Work and Pensions. For example, one woman described how "social just send you letters", whereas her adviser explained the *process* of claiming benefits and appealing; this explanation of the process helped her to be prepared, so that she did not panic when letters arrived from the DWP. Another woman explained how the CAB adviser helped her to keep a written record of the claims process:

> 'They send you a summary of what you've discussed and what you've done which is brilliant because then you've got a record of it, I just think they're excellent ... you can phone them up and say well I saw such and such a person on such and such a date, this is the reference, and it makes life so much easier. So, not like the DWP. You never speak to the same person twice.'

Being questioned

The experience of being questioned came up repeatedly in the interviews; people described being questioned through benefits claim forms, at medical assessments and at appeal tribunals. Just as interviewees often felt disempowered when they asked questions *of* institutions, they also felt disempowered and intimidated when they were questioned *by* institutions.

Unable to explain their situation

Interviewees described how the questions that they were asked in claim forms or medical examinations did not address their individual circumstances, but rather were "standardised" or "generic"; they had to "tick boxes" or give short answers to repetitive questions. They therefore felt that although they had to answer lots of questions, they were unable to fully explain their situations. Difficulties with claim forms were experienced not only by people with literacy problems or little education but also by people with higher levels of education. One woman, with a university education, summarised the experience when she said "they all want to know absolutely everything but not very much in the end". She also explained how her difficulties with the forms were exacerbated by her health problems which reduced her mental energy:

> 'A form is an official document yeah? Whereby you, as I say, you put your answers clearly and concisely and they're straight to the point ... it was the thought of, well it's going to take me a couple of hours to sit here and try and *write this out*, in *coherent* language ... and I just wasn't capable of doing it at the time.' [Her emphasis]

Being questioned by advisers

In contrast with their experiences of being questioned by institutions, interviewees in general found being questioned by advisers an empowering process. They felt that they were listened to, that they were not judged, and that their adviser's questions helped them to fully explain their circumstances. Only one interviewee described feeling judged in the past by advisers, although this was not the case with her current adviser.

Some interviewees explained how advisers helped them to complete claim forms by asking how they would deal with particular scenarios;

this helped them to think of things they had not put down in the form before.

'She didn't change the meanings [of the questions] but she would change the wording so as it would fit my situation.'

'She asked me questions I hadn't even really thought about...'

One woman who had tried for four years to claim a disability benefit, without any help from an adviser, described how she thought she had been very "narrow-minded" when she filled in the forms on her own. She had not put certain difficulties down on the form because she had not thought they were the sort of "disabled things" that were relevant to the claim. By contrast, her adviser had, as she put it, "gone into widescreen" and helped her to make a successful claim:

'Going to see [the adviser] she was able to put me in their [the DWP] mindset, but get into mine as well. So she brought the two elements together, put it on paper and job done.'

These descriptions support an understanding of advisers acting as translators, not in the sense of moving from one technical language to another, but rather putting 'two things together in such a way as to create a third, a new thing, with a meaning of its own' (Boyd White, 1990: 263). Such translation is important in helping claimants to participate fully in the claims process; in other words, helping clients to complete claim forms is not simply a question of helping clients to provide dry 'facts' but of helping clients to put together a full account of their illness or disability within the framework of the relevant law.

Lies and tricks

Some interviewees described how they experienced questioning by institutions as a test of their credibility or moral character. When their claims were unsuccessful they felt their answers to the questions had not been believed:

'What got me the most was when I had the letter … stopping it [her benefit payment], was just the fact that they don't believe me … and then I went to see the doctor, he said was it about the money, I said no, it's not about the money, it's they don't believe me, the problems I've got and it really cut me up.'

One interviewee described her appeal tribunal hearing as being like an interrogation in a magistrate's court during which she felt as if she was being sentenced for being ill. This experience was, in part, shaped by the advice given to her by her adviser who had said, when looking at the appeal papers "do you know they [the DWP] think you're lying?" The interviewee explained how in her next medical assessment she would therefore be more wary of the medical assessor's questions:

'I'll just be listening to more what they're actually saying to me you know because I'm, they're asking me questions, I'm answering them and not thinking you know, they're thinking I'm lying.'

This client therefore experienced questioning not as an exercise in the gathering of information but rather as a form of cross-examination. This experience was also reflected in some interviewees' descriptions of questions as trick questions, designed to trick them into saying something which would disqualify them from receiving the benefit. Questions were often viewed as trick questions when they were seen as repetitive.

'It was something on the form and they were asking you about your disability but then they asked you a question about how it affects your disability and then, then they twist it. It's the same kind of question they're asking you but they twist it … it's like trick questions do you know what I mean?'

Some interviewees believed that their advisers could protect them from such trick questions. For example, one man said his adviser could help him to "see through" trick questions on the claim forms and "cut to the chase". Another interviewee explained how the presence of the adviser at her tribunal hearing helped her to feel protected:

'I think them [the DWP] knowing that you've got somebody you know covering your back and going to these appeals with you it's a different thing than you going on your own do you know what I mean because they'll ask you a question and I look at her [the adviser] and oh they mean whatever do you know what I mean. Now if I was there on my own I'd be answering questions sometimes and didn't understand.'

Interpreters and questioning

A Somalian interviewee explained how she found the benefits claim process and appeal hearings difficult not only because of the number of questions she was asked but also because she could not be sure whether the interpreter was accurately conveying her answers to the questions. Similarly, she was not able to read questions on claim forms or the answers that the interpreter wrote down. Although interpreters are commonly understood as having a neutral role in which they translate exactly what is said, it has been shown that court interpreters play a far more active verbal role. For example, interpreters sometimes insert powerless forms of language into their interpretation, and on other occasions delete powerless forms which are in the source language (powerless language is a term used to describe a speaking style which, for example, uses 'hedge words' and answers questions with sentences which have a rising intonation [Berk-Seligson, 1990; Conley and O'Barr, 2005]). This is important because it has been shown that jurors are more likely to believe people who use powerful forms of language than people who use powerless forms (Conley and O'Barr, 2005). People who need to use an interpreter therefore experience an additional dimension of disempowerment when being questioned, compared with people who do not need an interpreter. However, this interviewee went on to say that the presence of her adviser helped her to feel confident at her appeal hearing, rather than nervous, because she trusted her adviser and knew that she would understand what was happening. The presence of the adviser therefore helped to lessen the anxieties that she had about the interpreter, despite the adviser also having to communicate with her through an interpreter

Gathering evidence

Many interviewees described how their advisers had emphasised the importance of gathering supporting evidence for their benefit claims and appeals. For example, one woman, having been turned down for ESA, was advised to keep a diary to record how her health problems affected her and to get a supporting letter from her son. She drew on this experience when she made a subsequent claim for a community care grant:

'so I thought right, past experience, you put it all down, the problems ... I said I'm sending the letters, you know a list of my medication ... then there's copy of the letter my son wrote for me ... that I used for the ESA. Then again for the OT [Occupational Therapist]...'

One man said his adviser had helped him to build up a "dossier" of written medical evidence, which he also described as a "stockpile of ammunition". He felt empowered by this evidence, describing himself as "forearmed" and "ready for them" in his second hearing.

However, obtaining written evidence from doctors is not necessarily a straightforward matter. For example, the man discussed above said his doctor had been unwilling to give him a copy of a letter that the doctor had been sent by the man's consultant. Another interviewee was pleased to get a supporting letter from her consultant but was uncertain as to how the consultant had come to send her this letter and was left wondering what would have happened if he had not done this. One woman could not get evidence from her GP about her mental health problems because she had not discussed them with her GP, believing that if she did so, she would be compelled to take medication which she did not want to do. This left her unable to 'prove' her condition. Interviewees therefore highlighted the precarious nature of obtaining evidence.

Conclusion

Previous research has shown that powerlessness is central to the experience of poverty and social exclusion. This is not to say that individuals experiencing poverty are passive victims, but rather that their ability to take action is constrained by a lack of resources and power. I have shown in this chapter how advice clients experience powerlessness in their interactions with the benefits system and four key ways in which the advice process helps to address this; advisers provide information about the broad benefits system and claims and appeal processes, help clients to communicate with institutions and uncover information about their claims, translate clients' stories of poor health and disability into accounts which meet the requirements of claims forms and tribunals, and help clients to gather evidence to support their claims. As described in Samuel Kirwan's chapter, one of the justifications made for removing legal aid from benefits advice in 2012 is that such advice is more practical than legal in nature. However, as clients highlight in their descriptions of advisers using books, the processes I have described in this chapter require advisers to have knowledge of the legal framework surrounding the benefits system; interviewees' accounts of the 'everyday' world of benefits advice suggest that the 'practical' and 'legal' are not readily separated but rather are inextricably linked.

GETTING FROM THE STORY OF A DISPUTE TO THE LAW

Emily Rose[*]

Introduction

What is your approach to giving employment advice? Responses to this question from specialist and generalist advisers, as well as solicitors working with the Citizens Advice service, emphasised a particular *process*. While the advice interview must start with the client's story, this initial narrative account represents only the first step; it is in what comes *after* this that the critical work of advice is achieved. In this chapter I explore how advisers move from the story of a dispute to the law. The practice engaged in by advisers is far more than simply an exercise in legal diagnostics. As I will explain, this represents just one stage. Other critical elements include teasing out the full range of relevant factual detail relating to the employment dispute, communicating the law to clients, and framing the law in terms of possible courses of action.

[*]   Emily Rose is a Lecturer in the School of Law at the University of Strathclyde. Her main area of research interest is labour law and social aspects of work and organisations. Emily's academic background spans both law and sociology and this interdisciplinary perspective informs the work she undertakes.

These latter aspects of the process take into account contextual issues beyond the immediate law, and involve consideration of the hurdles inherent in the Employment Tribunal process, the disposition of the client, and the level of support that the adviser can offer throughout the course of the dispute.

Gathering the story and identifying the law

The advisers in our study typically began the first advice session by giving clients space to talk freely about the problem they faced at work. As described in Samuel Kirwan's chapter, allowing them to tell their story often had the effect of putting the client at ease. But, crucially, it also commenced the first step of identifying the nature of the dispute.

It was important at this point to develop an understanding of the clients' account of events – to establish the chronological order of occurrences, the nature of the relationships between the parties involved, and details of who engaged in which actions (or inactions). Equally critical, though, was the need for advisers to broaden out the focus of the discussion. Advisers asked questions that aimed to guide clients' attention on matters relevant in law but not necessarily recognised by the client as being important. A commonplace example here are details of the actions (or inactions) on the part of the employer, which the adviser could then assess as constituting correct procedure or not. The questions asked by advisers could also unearth additional potential legal claims that the client may not have thought of or realised were possible (unpaid holiday pay is one typical example of something often overlooked by a client). Advisers spoke of this stage as 'digging around' or 'ferreting out' information – an attempt to capture all potentially relevant detail and unearth that which was not revealed by the client.

In most cases, in this initial advice meeting, advisers would also attempt to compile details of factual information relevant to the general operation of employment law. One adviser referred to this as developing the 'framework' in which the dispute took place. This 'framework', comprised of details such as where the client worked, the job they undertook, how long they had worked there, whether they were an employee or otherwise, and so on, allowed advisers to further identify appropriate categories of law that may apply to the clients' disputes.

What comes through in these accounts is the extent to which the relevant law, and possible basis for a claim, are not necessarily immediately apparent: it takes a careful process of investigation to determine these. Indeed, the full extent of the factual detail may only emerge over a course of interactions between adviser and client as the relevant evidence is accumulated and examined. One specialist employment adviser described how he spends the first few weeks of a dispute in what he calls 'fact finding mode'. Moreover, there may be intermediate steps that the client or the adviser on their behalf can pursue before the crystallisation of a potential claim. These actions can include writing a letter to an employer or raising a formal grievance with them. Such steps and their associated responses (or lack of them) on the part of the employer may take weeks or even months.

Gathering the story and identifying the law involved active roles on the part of both the client and the adviser. The client, after taking the initial step of approaching the CAB and relaying their narrative of the events experienced, was prompted to reiterate and elaborate upon various components of the narrative. Documentary evidence of the events was often procured. Advisers, for their part, while allowing clients space to communicate, are active in guiding the nature of information volunteered so that they can begin to align this with relevant law.

Communicating the law and framing possible courses of action

The second area of practice that is key in the process of moving from the story to the law is the task of outlining the relevant law to clients and framing possible courses of action for the client to take. Again, this is not as straightforward as merely describing the relevant legal framework and how this will apply to the client's situation.

In terms of communicating the law itself, advisers are mindful that many of their clients will have very limited knowledge of employment law. This may also be combined with low educational attainment and low levels of confidence about utilising such a formal institution. Thus advisers are aware of the risks of overwhelming clients with the complexity of employment law, of confusing them, or even of intimidating them. As a result of this, advisers typically sought to avoid any negative effects of communicating legal information by focusing on the specific aspect of the law or procedure that was immediately relevant to the client at that particular stage of the dispute, or by outlining the law in general terms instead of detailed specifics, or by focusing particularly on the practical steps that the adviser and client needed to engage in as opposed to the technical detail.

If these techniques display an awareness of legal knowledge as a potential *inhibitor* of action, advisers also described a contrasting view of knowledge as *empowering* clients. One specialist employment adviser, for example, viewed communicating the relevant law to clients as necessary to making the law accessible; removing the mystery from the legal process would render it less intimidating for clients. Thus the adviser considered that this could have the effect of encouraging a client to pursue their case. Likewise, a generalist adviser spoke of the importance of directing clients to the considerable array of information available on the Advice Guide and ACAS websites. His view was that most clients were very interested in being able to explore this in greater detail to better inform themselves of their situation (as discussed in Morag McDermont's chapter, this view of the role of the Citizens Advice website is one that the service itself is moving away from).

Implicit in outlining the relevant law is the need to make an assessment of the merits of a client's claim. This requires objectivity on the part of the adviser, something which they acknowledged can be difficult at times. Both the client and adviser may feel that a real injustice has occurred. But this does not necessarily translate into a strong basis for a claim against an employer. While an adviser may empathise with the client, it was noted that giving them a sense of hope is ultimately fruitless. One solicitor described how this had happened to her and that she had learnt from it:

> 'If it's weak, it's better for you to just say so and let them move on, than you drag this out when you really knew it was weak – but you feel sorry for them or you let them talk you into it, and then they have a year or two years of this hanging over them.'

When it came to translating relevant law into possible courses of action advisers were acutely aware of the practical realities of actually pursuing claims in the Employment Tribunal, difficulties discussed in Nicole Busby's and Eleanor Kirk's contributions to this book. For some advisers, this made this stage of the client-adviser interaction difficult. One specialist employment adviser noted that "A lot of my conversations to do with employment law are negative and you have to be realistic – it's not my job to mislead people, so you have to tell them what the hurdles are going to be."

Alongside advisers' explanations of the hurdles involved in the Employment Tribunal process was a sensitivity to the associated *stress* of pursuing a claim in this way. A solicitor stated: "I know that [the Employment Tribunal] try, and they do try, to make it as stress free as possible but they can't make it stress free, it's just impossible to make it stress free." Advisers sought to explain to clients that, in practice, taking a claim to the Employment Tribunal requires a degree of determination, grit and psychological strength. This underpinned, to a degree, the way in which advisers framed possible courses of action to clients. One solicitor noted:

> 'there are some clients who are in tears the whole time you're speaking to them when they're going over the situation, and I am reluctant to go ahead with clients in that situation just because if they find difficulty dealing with the stress of speaking to me, the stress of appearing in a tribunal is going to be very, very high.'

The solicitor would not refuse to help them if they did want to proceed. However, he would ask them to take some time to consider again their planned course of action.

Clients' ability to deal with stress of the dispute also came to the fore in circumstances in which the CAB providing advice could only offer limited support to their client – situations which frequently occurred due to resource constraints. When deciding upon whether to allocate further adviser time to these cases, advisers would take account not only of the capability of the client to undertake aspects of the case themselves, but would also assess the actual legal merit of the case and the possibility of achieving a positive outcome.

The stage at which advisers communicate the law and frame possible courses of action is critical in terms of the potential to empower clients. Of course all advisers aim to empower clients. However, the nature of employment law – its complexity, what is deemed to be inappropriate in the employment relationship and what falls outside of this, and its procedural elements – can make this difficult. Relaying knowledge of the law to clients, for example, while often assumed to be positive for clients, is done so carefully and thoughtfully by advisers. Likewise, the framing of possible next steps takes into account the contextual reality such as the personal support and stability of clients and the degree of professional support an adviser can offer. The aspect of the process, then, is nuanced, with the client very much placed at the centre.

Conclusion

At first glance, providing employment advice, at least for those skilled in the matter, may appear a fairly straightforward matter. It would involve identifying the legally relevant facts and applying the law. However, when we frame the idea of 'getting to the law' in terms of eliciting the full picture, communicating the law to clients and framing possible courses of action, certain complexities come into play. CAB advisers are typically dealing with clients who are stressed from their employment problems and who may also be experiencing associated financial difficulties. Moreover, many of their clients lack experience of employment law and may have levels low of education. Advisers skilfully take account of these factors, as well as the challenges of going through the Employment Tribunal process, and provide sensitive and realistic advice for their clients.

"ADVICE ON THE LAW BUT NOT LEGAL ADVICE SO MUCH": WEAVING LAW AND LIFE INTO DEBT ADVICE

Samuel Kirwan[*]

Second unsupervised interview. Client had come in with water debt, but then mentioned that she had an unpaid Council Tax Bill. She was visibly upset when I explained the importance of engaging with this. Had a sudden, strong feeling of how easy it is to end up in this position, where outgoings are so much more than income, where it's impossible to imagine how you can afford to meet ongoing bills, and have difficulty opening the post. (Field Diary)

[*] Samuel Kirwan is a research fellow at the University of Warwick who worked on the New Sites of Legal Consciousness project. He is particularly interested in the process of money advice, and the moral language of debt and credit that surrounds it, and has a longstanding interest in the concept of the commons.

Introduction

My diary of participating in the Citizens Advice training programme is littered with these experiences. Notes on Debt Relief Order procedure are followed by my own worries about forgotten credit cards or the Council Tax Bill – debt in the abstract intertwining with debt as personal anxiety. We are used to thinking of debt as a question of morality (I am frequently reminded by friends that both Swedish and German hold the same word for 'debt' as for 'guilt'), or of time: debt as the purchasing of today's consumption with tomorrow's labour. It is unusual to think of debt as a *legal* question. Yet it is through debt that many people will become enmeshed within the reaches of law, whether being forced to engage with the power of a contract or to question the nature of ownership. What defines *different* debts, as opposed to debt generally, are the legal framings that shape, among other things, how, when and by whom they can be enforced and collected.

I will explore here what debt advice tells us about how 'law' and 'life' are intertwined in the practice of advice. This intertwining, I argue, has important implications for the ongoing role of advice in the context of an assumption, presented in a Ministry of Justice paper that preceded the Legal Aid, Sentencing and Punishment of Offenders Act (LASPO), that volunteer advisers merely provide the public with 'practical' information (MoJ, 2010). I will focus on the question raised by this assumption: is there a difference between the advice they give and formal 'legal advice', and does this difference matter?

The debt advice process

From our interviews and diaries of the Citizens Advice training programme, trainees noted that, compared to the perils of negotiating the labyrinthine intricacies of the UK benefits system, debt advice appears reasonably straightforward.[1] The debt training pack introduces a flowchart for debt queries, one that begins, in the rectangle at the top of the chart, with an initial exploration of the client's circumstances, following which the chart splits in two, defining two strands of work.

On the left the process moves through an identification of emergencies, separation of debts and assignment of priority, of which more below, to each particular debt. On the right, the drawing up of household budget sheets through the Common Financial Statement (CFS). The flows join together in an exploration of various options.

Yet, in contrast to the simplicity implied by this flow diagram, one money specialist made a claim for money advice to be the most complicated of advice areas given the extent to which the adviser must allow the client to make their own decisions. What this claim reflects, I argue, is the complexity of the emotional relationship between adviser and client that forms the fabric of the debt advice process. Described across our interviews are the particular forms of attachment and detachment that characterise debt advice; seeking to form a relationship between the client and their budget but ultimately being detached from the contents of this budget, and never being able to fully know if the client will stick to it. More than any other area the labour carried out by debt advisers shifts emphasis from the client as a bureaucratic entity composed through legal frameworks to the individual as a set of emotional attachments in the everyday.

The boundaries of 'legal' advice

I argue that it is these dimensions of the practice of advice that can explain the different responses advisers gave to our questions of whether they are carrying out 'legal' advice. A first interesting point from responses to these questions was that there were those who were certain either that the Citizens Advice service *does* give legal advice, or that it does not. The first perspective was typically described through an imagining of advice work as the communication of information *derived from legal frameworks*. It was clearly articulated by an adviser with a legal background who, discussing the misunderstandings of advice held by clients, noted: "When you say legal advice to people they think solicitors, barristers, wigs, gowns and formal letters." They don't realise, she went on, that "what they are coming in to see is actually legal advice" (Claire, Specialist adviser).

Where participants stated clearly that they do *not* give 'legal advice', it was sometimes in the context of noting the *limits* to what can be advised upon, indicated by the 'warning triangle' on AdviserNet; for some of our participants this symbol specifically indicated a 'legal issue'. For others the distinction was bound to the professional differences between advisers and solicitors, whether related to the different forms of knowledge they hold, or the ways in which these different actors carry different levels of responsibility for the information they impart.

However, these expressions of certainty were the exception. For the most part the issue of whether advice is 'legal' was recognised as being 'a difficult question to answer' (Greg, Specialist adviser). Considerable ambiguities and conflicts arose as participants considered the *practice* of advice, and what it was advisers were *doing* to the information – widely understood to be derived from legal frameworks – that formed the backbone of their work. Indicative of this conflicted approach was the description of the work by one adviser: "It is advice on law but not legal advice so much". This, the adviser continued, could be explained on the basis that "we can only really advise them on how law relates to the issue that we've got", as opposed to "delving into bits of law that I just don't understand" (Greg, Specialist adviser). Yet elsewhere advisers noted that they did hold considerable legal knowledge and expertise beyond what is contained in the Citizens Advice information systems. Thus one group discussion became focused upon the extent to which advisers could *interpret* the law. Several participants thought that, in contrast to their work, solicitors were able to predict a judge or make a statement on the strength of a case, one stating that "we don't get involved in the tactics" (Geoff, Generalist adviser). Another argued against this, citing employment as one area "of law where I think we can be a bit more helpful, a bit more tactical" (Enid, Specialist adviser).

What these examples show is both the importance for advisers of distinguishing their work from formal legal advice, and the frequency with which advisers questioned the particular points of distinction through which this difference might be explained. In order to better explain this relationship between advice and 'the law', we need to focus further upon the actual practice of advice and the question of how it is that legal frameworks are engaged with, communicated and explained in different circumstances. As such, before making a proposition for how we might think of this relationship, we will turn to how advisers described these different forms of advice practice and the role of 'the law' therein.

The 'relational work' of advice

A key goal of the project was to understand advisers' views on *what advice is*, and what it requires, beyond the passing on of information. Some responded to these questions by stressing the advice process as entirely *simple*:

> 'We don't advise anybody diddly squat, we give them their options and we help them with the implications of pursuing those individual options.' (Adrian, Manager)

In this respect participants would often stress the difference between advice work and counselling, and the ways in which the former is "a lot less emotionally involved" (Miriam, Specialist adviser). Yet, at the same time, and often in the same interviews, it was recognised that this was only half the story, and that there were a range of 'basic counselling skills' (Claire, Specialist adviser) often employed by advisers. This recognition of there being an *emotional* and *relational* dimension to advice, defining different ways in which advisers seek to engage with and transform the client, is key, I argue, to understanding what effective advice is; it was these subtle variations that advisers emphasised when describing their expertise. I term this work the 'relational labour' of advice, emphasising the extent to which the work carried out by the adviser cannot be separated from the relationship with the client.

I divide the 'relational labour' of advice workers into three categories: facilitating understanding, creating clarity and creating ownership, noting in each case its importance to the work of debt advice.

Facilitating understanding

Advisers described the importance of knowing how to enable clients to use the knowledge they already had or that was readily available to them. They described how, by asking the correct questions, and establishing a basis in which the client feels safe and trusted, clients can work through their issues and fully understand the information being presented to them. What was interesting about this work was the emphasis on legal information being already available, but inaccessible.

A specific form of this facilitation was described as taking place in those situations where a client's emotional state led them to focus on their 'rights' at the expense of the practicalities and consequences of certain actions. Advisers described how, while clients, to some extent, understood their rights (or that they had rights), they would need to engage in a difficult balancing task of explaining what action a landlord, or employer, could legally take if the client did indeed decide to act upon their 'right' to report a broken gate or lodge a grievance related to workplace bullying. One adviser described needing to state to the client that:

> 'You are absolutely right, you are well within your rights to do that, but this is the other side, this is what they can do so you have to now go away and think very carefully of what level you want to throw this back at them.' (Annette, Specialist adviser)

In the context of debt advice, this work of facilitating understanding can be seen to take place in the drawing up of the CFS. The spreadsheet forms the central plank of the debt process, allowing both for an organisation of the household's financial situation and for communication with and representation to creditors. While it is no more than the presentation of information provided by the client, namely their different forms of income and expenditure, it is in the relational labour of negotiating, organising and representing this information that the client is able to gain clarification of where they are and what they can do.

Creating clarity

For one trainee the creation of clarity was akin to a removal of emotions from a situation:

> 'There is an awful lot of emotion involved, so what you need to try and do is try and take the emotions from any dealings'. (Steve, Trainee)

In debt cases particularly, frequently discussed in this respect was the importance of knowing how to deal with clients for whom the weight of worry, anxiety or shame was hindering their ability to deal with their problems. Advisers note in such cases the manner in which debts can overpower life – how the sight of letters building up beneath the letterbox or the fear of bailiffs aroused by reference to 'debt collectors', can remove a client's capacity to engage with their situation. Yet advisers recognised that clearing these feelings away required attention to the emotional situation of the client; it was noted, for example, that effective advice can only happen once the initial work of establishing a 'rapport' between adviser and client is achieved.

It is the role of *law* in creating this clarity that I wish to focus on here. In debt advice this is firstly achieved in the communication of the difference between 'priority' and 'non-priority' debts. This distinction, used across the advice sector, simply describes the difference between those debts whose non-payment can lead to the loss of home (mortgage, rent), liberty (council tax, court fees) and essential services (gas and electricity) and those that do not (principally consumer debts). The description of the difference between priority and non-priority debts, and how this is rooted in law, can be a way of cutting through what is often a crowded field of 'emotional attachments'.[2] By appealing to the legal distinctions that constitute the priority/non-priority divide, advisers seek to begin a new set of emotional attachments between the client and their debts. Separated into different sets of options and consequences, debts can be moved from a space of anxiety and fear to one of a clear, known future, allowing the client the emotional space to deal with other issues they are facing.

Creating ownership

The emotional interventions of advisers were recognised most clearly in discussions over the client who 'just doesn't care about it' and the need for them to take 'ownership' (Bruce, Specialist adviser). Two advisers who specialised in debt work elaborated upon this 'difficulty' through a distinction between 'blasé' clients and those who are overwrought with emotion. One adviser described experiencing no duty to impress "rights and responsibilities" on a client who is "frightened because they owe £400 to somebody that they can't afford to pay", whereas "you don't treat the ones that are a bit blasé about it in a nasty way but you can be a bit more forthright with them" (Margaret, Generalist adviser). As another stated:

> 'I can find it quite healthy if somebody comes to me with debt problems in tears, because it shows they care. The worse type of person is somebody that just doesn't care about it and just wants it sorted, because working with them is more difficult.' (Henry, Focus group of advisers)

Conclusion

I will finish with a proposition for this relationship between advice work and 'law', and why it matters. The interventions made by advisers into the understandings of their clients rely, I argue, upon a labour in which advisers understand how to create and manage a distinction between an imagining of 'the law' and the life of the client. To create clarity, attachment or ownership relies upon knowing when and how to move between legal frameworks and the everyday life of the client. Thus, while the material backbone of the work is 'legal', the work itself is not so easily classified. What constitutes advice work *as work*, as opposed to the passing on of information, are the various ways in which advisers understand how to weave 'law' into the advice interview. Thus, as *work*, its importance lies in a certain *externality* to law.

To return to the government proposition made at the outset of this chapter, to equate this work with 'practical advice', implying individuals with discrete problems that can be sorted through a straightforward practice of information provision, misunderstands the skills advisers hold and their relationship to the law. Not only are problems rarely discrete, meaning that advisers must address the subject as a whole, investigating multiple and interwoven problems, but individuals will come to this advice with certain attachments, preconceived assumptions and emotional states. The task of the adviser is not only to pass on the relevant legal information in a particular area, but to assess 'the law' *from outside* the law.

Notes

[1] My own diary of the training programme marvelled at how an area that was so obscure to me could be so clearly laid out. This was rarely the case in my initial casework as a trainee.

[2] The work of Deville (2012) has highlighted the practices used by debt collection agencies – agencies that purchase debt from creditors and other agencies and seek to recoup it – and how these hinge upon achieving an emotional connection between the client and their debts that prioritises *their* debt above all others.

10
REFLECTIONS ON ADVISING IN AUSTERITY

John Clarke[*]

This book has explored the conditions, processes and practices of advising in austerity and this last chapter pulls out some of the key themes and issues from across the book. Perhaps the most significant theme concerns the pace and scale of the economic, social and political changes that form the context in which advice work is undertaken. In one sense, this is a banal observation – everyone who works in Citizens Advice has a direct grasp of the deepening social dislocations that have generated increasing demand for support and advice. During the last decade in particular, the range of those changes (and the resulting demand) has been particularly striking and a growing body of research testifies to the social consequences of 'austerity' politics and policies (for example Garthwaite, 2016). This study adds to that body of work in a distinctive way, revealing how particular individuals are experiencing the dislocations and seeking to find ways through them – whether it is Lucy's problems in finding support for being

[*] John Clarke is a Professor Emeritus in Social Policy at the Open University and also teaches at Central European University in Budapest. He has written extensively about welfare states, public services and citizenship. For many years he was a CAB trustee.

homeless or Brian's encounters with a bullying employer. These are both individual experiences of troubles in austerity-driven Britain, but they are also exemplary moments of how policies have changed the sorts of public support available to resolve such private troubles. Both Lucy and Brian experienced the difficulties of trying to find support in a world of underfunded services (both public and voluntary). The book helps us to see 'austerity' as connecting three things: an ideology or way of thinking that legitimates particular sorts of policy changes, the profoundly unequal economic and social impact of contemporary transformations, and the assault on public spending and public services that has been underpinned by claims about the need for austerity. Citizens Advice is one of the critical places where all these things come together in the form of private troubles and the efforts to remedy them.

This brings a second significant issue into view because Citizens Advice, like many other organisations, is simultaneously trying to respond to the increasing demand for help and trying to cope with a turbulent policy environment in the face of shrinking funding. Both the national organisations and the local bureaux are expending increasing amounts of their organisational attention and effort on coping with this turbulence and trying to invent new ways of supporting themselves. Bureau managers, as we saw earlier, face pressures to become more 'entrepreneurial', finding new funding sources, bidding for new projects, and dealing with the demands and constraints that new funding sources bring with them. Bureaux face conflicting injunctions – to be more 'competitive' (winning bids against other potential providers) and to be more 'collaborative' (working in partnership with other organisations). They are also (as Chapter Three showed) facing pressures to 'modernise' and change their ways of working as the future for public services becomes defined as 'digital'. At the same time, voluntary organisations like Citizens Advice experience increasing regulatory pressures – to be more accountable, to keep out of politics, to deliver 'value for money', for example - and each of these brings new burdens and constraints. This is a fearsome nexus of pressures that place new stresses on organisations, take up managerial time and energy, and require those working in such organisations, particularly as volunteers, to adapt and adopt new ways of working. Voluntary organisations became a fraught focal point of the multiple pressures and expectations contained in the assumptions of the 'Big Society', espoused by then Prime Minister David Cameron – not least the belief that voluntary organisations could not just supplement public services, but could replace them.

Nowhere is this more evident than in the field of employment law. The book illuminates the ways in which what was always a challenging field of work for Citizens Advice has become increasingly difficult.

The research behind this book emerged from an interest in how legality and the assumptions and practices of the law intersected with, and were experienced in, areas of everyday life (Ewick and Silbey, 1998). Three important issues have stood out here. First, people in the UK have faced increasing difficulties accessing formal legal processes as new barriers are constructed. The reduction of legal aid provision and the charging of fees for some processes combine to put new material barriers between people and the law. Such barriers intensify the felt distance between ordinary people and the law – where the law is perceived as alien or not for 'people like us' (and is associated with a sense of powerlessness). Second, the research here points to the connections and disjunctions between people's sense of 'justice' (what is and is not fair) and the realm of law. We have seen people seeking legal remedies (at Employment Tribunals for example) for felt injustices and then finding a gap opening up between their sense of justice and the law's categories and judgments. This points to important questions for further investigation (where do ideas of justice come from? What are their social and political consequences?); for political and policy action (how might justice and law be reconciled?) and for those working in the advice field (how can we align people's desires for justice and their encounters with the law? How can we make justice more accessible and meaningful?). These last questions about practice also point to what the book has to say about the *work* of advice.

At the heart of what takes place in the advice process are acts of 'translation' in which advisers mediate between everyday lives and the framings, understandings and languages of law and policy (Freeman,

2009; McDermont, 2013). This research shows that this translation is always a double process: on one side, advisers have to work to translate the experiences and troubles of the person seeking help into the categories and framings of the law; on the other side, advisers must translate the law back into the life of the person seeking help. Without such 'translation back', people will be unable to make choices, exercise some degree of control or act on their troubles. This (as we saw in Chapter Nine) is a critical moment in the advice process – without it, people are merely receiving information. The moments of understanding, clarity and ownership that Samuel Kirwan describes can only come about through effective translations – of troubles into law, and of law into meaningful possibilities for action. This enriches the understanding of translation in studies of law, which have tended to focus on the first moment (translating things into legal framings) but here we can see how important the second aspect is. Equally importantly, the visibility given to 'relational work' as part of the advice process brings something important to studies of translation which have tended to neglect such dimensions.

Citizens Advice is, of course, not just about 'advice' but also raises a question of what citizenship might mean. The study asked volunteers, workers and managers who they thought the citizen in Citizens Advice might refer to. Often, they said they had not thought about it, but when pressed, there was one phrase that recurred frequently - 'anyone who comes through the door':

> 'I personally think it's anybody who walks through the door for advice is a citizen in Citizens Advice Bureaux. So it is anyone within society who basically needs our help, who comes through the door.' (Rebecca: Specialist adviser)

This is, of course, some distance from the legal definition of the citizen (and the accompanying eligibility for citizenship rights). Instead, people from Citizens Advice were at pains to stress the principle of openness, refusing to identify any barriers to eligibility. They certainly knew that there were other, more formal, definitions of citizenship but regularly returned to the way that the needs of 'anyone who comes through the door' overrode such definitions:

> 'No, the advice is open to anyone really who needs the advice because, at the end of the day, everybody who has come to the UK and it doesn't matter for whatever reason or for however long, if they're in a situation where they need help, they use the service. From this point of view, it doesn't really matter if they've arrived last month and found themselves in a difficult situation .... so to have a service like this that's open to anyone is absolutely amazing and can only be a good thing.' (Alexandra: Generalist adviser in a semi-urban bureau)

Such comments point to the continuing social and political importance of ideas of citizenship that go beyond the current narrowing of rights, benefits and access in the UK (for example Dwyer and Wright, 2014). They are certainly of practical importance – for those who receive support (and for those who provide it). But we think that they are also of wider value: they demonstrate ways of thinking and acting in a citizenly fashion that are urgently needed. They stand out against the dominant tendencies of the period, the narrowing of citizenship, the shrinking of its rights and the increasing difficulty of claiming or being able to enforce such rights.

Like other voluntary organisations, Citizens Advice occupies an ambiguous space - such service-providing organisations are highly valued (not least because voluntary provision tends to be cheaper than public services), and they embody the Big Society principle of mutual support rather than the Big State. But organisations such as Citizens Advice also do campaigning work - and are staffed by people who hold views about citizenship that may differ from those currently dominant. This is one reason why voluntary organisations (in the UK and in many other places) have come under increasing pressure to 'keep out of politics' (Clarke, forthcoming). It is clear that Citizens Advice provides a space where alternative conceptions of citizenship and relationships between citizens have been kept alive in principle and in practice.

But the difficult question is: can these alternatives be sustained? This is not just a matter of whether the ideas persist in people's heads, but recognising that they emerge from, and are put into practice within, particular settings, patterns of relationships, organisational cultures and norms of conduct. These supports and settings matter for how people are able to think and act – what Shannon Jackson (2011), writing about the contexts of public art, calls the collective *infrastructure* of being able to think and behave in significant ways. The growing pressures on Citizens Advice put this ethos – and the infrastructure that sustains it – at risk.

The future is perilous, both for those who would use Citizens Advice and for the service itself. The experience of constantly striving to do more with less is not sustainable – either for the organisations or the people who work in them. We have already seen a decline in the number of bureaux through closures and mergers. There is a potential spiral of declining capacity, the displacement of a generalist service by targeted work attached to specific funding, a rise in the non-face-to-face forms of service provision (telephone and online advice) in place of the immediate encounters that volunteers and clients seem to value highly. Such changes challenge the infrastructure that has sustained citizenly ways of thinking and behaving. They do so at a dangerous moment, when the wider dynamics of social and economic dislocation create dangerous times for citizens and citizenly conduct.

REFERENCES

Abbott, B. (1998) 'The emergence of a new industrial relations actor—the role of the citizens' Advice Bureaux?' *Industrial Relations Journal*, 29(4): 257-69.

Balmer, N.J., Smith, M., Denvir, C. and Patel, A. (2012) 'Just a phone call away: is telephone advice enough?', *Journal of Social Welfare and Family Law*, 34(1): 63-85.

Beatty, C., Foden, M., McCarthy, L. and Reeve, K. (2015) *Benefit Sanctions and Homelessness: A Scoping Report*, London: Crisis.

Beecroft, A. (2011) *Report on Employment Law*, London: Department of Business, Innovation and Skills.

Berk-Seligson, S. (1990) *The Bilingual Courtroom: Court Interpreters in the Judicial Process*, Chicago: University of Chicago Press.

BIS (Department of Business, Innovation and Skills) (2010) *Employment Relations Research Series No. 107, Findings from the Survey of Employment Tribunal Applications 2008* (March 2010), London: Department of Business, Innovation and Skills.

BIS (Department of Business, Innovation and Skills) (2011) *Resolving Workplace Disputes: A Consultation* (January 2011), London: Department of Business, Innovation and Skills.

BIS (Department of Business, Innovation and Skills) (2012), *Ending the Employment Relationship: Consultation*, London: Department of Business, Innovation and Skills.

BIS (Department of Business, Innovation and Skills) (2013a) *Findings from the Survey of Employment Tribunal Applications 2013: Research Series No. 177*, London: Department of Business, Innovation and Skills.

BIS (Department of Business, Innovation and Skills) (2013b) *Ending the Employment Relationship: Government Response to Consultation*, Department of Business, Innovation and Skills.

BIS (Department of Business, Innovation and Skills) (2013c) *Payment of Tribunal Awards: 2013 Study* [IFF Research], London: Department of Business, Innovation and Skills.

Blyth, M. (2013) *Austerity: The History of a Dangerous Idea*, Oxford: Oxford University Press.

Bourdieu, P. (2010) *Sociology is a Martial Art – Political Writings by Pierre Bourdieu*, New York and London: The New Press.

Boyd White, J. (1990) *Justice as Translation*, Chicago: University of Chicago Press.

Buck, A., Smith, M., Sidaway, J. and Scanlan, L. (2010) *Piecing It Together: Exploring One-Stop Shop Legal Service Delivery in Community Legal Advice Centres*, London: Legal Services Commission.

Cabinet Office (2012) 'Not-for-profit advice services in England', [Report], London: The Cabinet Office.

Cabinet Office (2016) 'Government announces new clause to be inserted into grant agreements' [Webpage], www.gov.uk/government/news/government-announces-new-clause-to-be-inserted-into-grant-agreements.

Citizens Advice (2016) 'Introduction to the Citizens Advice service' [Webpage], www.citizensadvice.org.uk/about-us/how-citizens-advice-works/who-we-are-and-what-we-do/introduction-to-the-citizens-advice-service/.

Citizens Advice Scotland (CAS) (2014) *Fair Enough? Protecting Scotland's Workers from Unfair Treatment* [Summary version of a report by Citizens Advice Scotland], Edinburgh: Citizens Advice Scotland.

Citizens Advice Scotland (CAS) (2016) 'About us' [Webpage], www.cas.org.uk/about-us.

Citron, J. (1989) *Citizens Advice Bureaux: For the Community, by the Community*, London: Pluto Press

Clarke, J. (forthcoming) 'Contesting civil society; contesting politics: a conjunctural view of the antagonisms of civil society', *Political Geography*.

REFERENCES

Clarke, J. and Newman, J. (2012) 'The alchemy of austerity', *Critical Social Policy*, 32(3): 299-319.

Cobb, S. (2013) 'Legal aid reform: its impact on family law', *Journal of Social Welfare and Family Law*, 35(1): 3-19.

Conley, J.M. and O'Barr, W.M. (2005) *Just Words: Law, Language and Power*, Chicago: University of Chicago Press.

Cooney, R. (2016) 'Commons motion urges government to reconsider anti-lobbying clause' [Webpage], www.thirdsector.co.uk/commons-motion-urges-government-reconsider-anti-lobbying-clause/policy-and-politics/article/1385085.

Deville, J. (2012) 'Generating market attachments; consumer credit debt collection and the capture of affect', *Journal of Cultural Economy*, 5(4): 423-439.

Dickens, L. (2000) 'Doing more with less: ACAS and individual conciliation' in Brown, W. and Towers, B. (eds) *Employment Relations in Britain: Twenty-Five Years of the Advisory, Conciliation and Arbitration Service*, Oxford: Blackwell.

Dickens, L. (ed) (2012) *Making Employment Rights Effective*, Oxford: Hart.

Downer, M., Harding, C., Ghezelayagh, S., Fu, E. and Gkiza, M. (2015) *Research Paper: Evaluation of ACAS Early Conciliation 2015*, London: Acas.

Dwyer, P.J. and Wright, S. (2014) 'Universal Credit, ubiquitous conditionality and its implications for social citizenship', *Journal of Poverty and Social Justice*, 22(1): 27-35.

Evans, B. and McBride, S. (eds) (forthcoming) *Austerity: The Lived Experience*, Toronto: University of Toronto Press.

Ewick, P. and Silbey, S. (1998) *The common place of law: stories from everyday life*, Chicago, IL: University of Chicago Press.

Freeman, R. (2009) 'What is "translation"?', *Evidence and Policy*, 5(4): 429-447.

Garthwaite, K. (2016) *Hunger Pains: Life inside Foodbank Britain*, Bristol: Policy Press.

Genn, H. (1999) *Paths to Justice*, Oxford: Hart.

Hepple, B. (2012) 'Agency enforcement of workplace equality', in Dickens, L. (ed) *Making Employment Rights Effective*, Oxford: Hart.

Hynes, S. (2013) *Austerity Justice*, London: Legal Action Group.

Jackson, S. (2011) *Social Works: Performing Art, Supporting Publics*, New York and London: Routledge.

Jones, R. (2010) 'Learning beyond the state: the pedagogical spaces of the CAB service', *Citizenship Studies*, 14(6): 725-738.

Karol Burks, B. (2015) 'Our new approach to digital advice' [Webpage], http://alphablog.citizensadvice.org.uk/2015/05/how-we-approach-advice-content/.

Kirwan, S., McDermont, M. and Clarke, J. (2016) 'Imagining and practising citizenship in austere times', *Citizenship Studies*, 20(6-7): 764-78.

Levitas, R. (2012) 'The just's umbrella: austerity and the Big Society in Coalition policy and beyond', *Critical Social Policy*, 32(3): 320-342.

Maclean, M. and Eekelaar, J. (2016) *Lawyers and Mediators: The Brave New World of Services for Separating Families*, Oxford: Hart.

Mayo, M., Koessl, G., Scott, M. and Slater, I. (2014) *Access to Justice for Disadvantaged Communities*, Bristol: Policy Press.

McDermont, M. (2013) 'Acts of translation: UK advice agencies and the creation of matters-of-public-concern', *Critical Social Policy*, 33(2): 218-42.

MoJ (Ministry of Justice) (2010) *Proposals for the Reform of Legal Aid in England and Wales* [Consultation paper 12/10], London: Ministry of Justice.

MoJ (Ministry of Justice) (2011) *Charging Fees in the Employment Tribunal and the Employment Appeal Tribunal*, London: Ministry of Justice.

MoJ (Ministry of Justice) (2012) *Charging Fees in the Employment Tribunals and Employment Appeal Tribunal: Response to Consultation*, London: Ministry of Justice.

Moorhead, R. (2001) 'Third way regulation? Community legal services partnerships', *The Modern Law Review*, 64(4): 543-562.

NAPO (2014) *The Impact of Legal Aid Cuts on Family Justice* [Report], London: NAPO.

NSLC (New Sites of Legal Consciousness) (2011) 'ERC starting grant research proposal' [Web document], www.bristol.ac.uk/media-library/sites/law/migrated/documents/newsitesfull.pdf.

NSLC (New Sites of Legal Consciousness) (2016) 'Advice agencies: New Sites of Legal Consciousness' [Webpage], www.bristol.ac.uk/law/research/centres-themes/aanslc/.

Ofcom (2012) *Communications Market Report 2012* [Research document], London: OFCOM.

O'Hara, E. (2011) *Shifting Channels: Housing Advice and the Growth of Digitisation* [Policy briefing], London: Shelter.

Peck, J. (2012) 'Austerity urbanism', *City: Analysis of Urban Trends, Culture, Theory, Policy, Action*, 16(6): 626–655.

Pollert, A. (2010) 'The lived experience of isolation for vulnerable workers facing workplace grievances in 21st-century Britain', *Economic and Industrial Democracy*, 31(1): 62–92.

Power, M. (1997) *The Audit Society: Rituals of Verification*, Oxford: Oxford University Press.

Royal Commission on Trade Unions and Employers' Associations (1968) 'Report of the Royal Commission on Trade Unions and Employers' Associations [The Donovan Report]', Cmnd 3623, HMSO.

Standing, G. (2011) *The Precariat – The New Dangerous Class*, London: Bloomsbury Academic.

The Law Society (2011) *Missing Millions* [Report], London: The Law Society.

TNS BMRB (2015) *Down the Line: The Future Role of Digital Housing Advice and Support* [Report], London: Shelter.

Wood, L. and Rose, E. (2014) 'The Citizens Advice experience of Employment Tribunal fees', Presentation given to the workshop, 'Employment Tribunal Fees: Evidencing the Impact', Glasgow 2014.

Wren-Lewis, J. (2015) 'The austerity con', *London Review of Books*, 37(4): 9–11.

Yates, S.J. (2015) '"Digital-by-default": reinforcing exclusion through technology' in Foster, F., Brunton, A., Deeming, C. and Haux, T. (eds) *In Defence of Welfare 2*, Bristol: Policy Press.

INDEX